ACKNOWLEDGMENTS

HEARTFELT THANKS TO the many authors who have allowed their work to be reprinted in this book. A version of "The Road Trip" by J.B. MacKinnon originally appeared under the title "Driving to This Point in History" in the Winter 2010 issue of Adbusters. Deborah Campbell's "Into the Lair of the White Bear" was originally published in the March 2008 issue of Canadian Geographic and Scott Russell Sanders "Settling Down" originally appeared under the title "Staying Put" in Orion magazine, Vol 11, No 1 (Winter 1992). Jake MacDonald's "The Commissioner" originally appeared in his 2005 book With The Boys and Susan Olding's essay, "Such Good Girls" is excerpted from her book Pathologies: A Life in Essays.

None of this work would be possible without the support of our 182 Kickstarter backers. Many of them could have easily bought themselves a romantic dinner for two (or a box set of Cicero's collected works) with the amount of money they pledged to our campaign, and we are ever grateful. Their names follow.

T.B.

THE KICKSTARTERS

J.B. MacKinnon
Bonnie Craig
Lauren and Matthew Hornor
Ronald Nimchuk
Fred and Mary Paranchych
Matt O'Grady
Robert Bridge
Barbara Murphy-Bridge
Jeffrey Hutchings
Elenora & Mike McGhee
Katrina Craig
Michele Bridge
Anne Kaye
Yuko Shibata
Trevor Boytinck
David Ng
Katrina Carroll-Foster
Eve Rickert
Greg Bole
Julie Kalmar
Geoff Bannoff
Jill Blaser
Chris Poskitt
Glen Kalmar
Catherine Bargen
Wade Papin
Morgan Burris
Christian Amott
Carla Olson
Sandi Kalmar
Johnny Bolton
Jeff Magnusson
Marie Irving
Björn Friedrich
Aline Lacey

Twila Mills
Alison Palmer
Amber Sessions
Shana Johnstone
Brian Mills
Michael Markwick
Marsha Williams
Brian Payton
Harv Phandal
Adele Weder
Dan Pez
Yoo-Mi Lee
Cassandra Bridge
Christine Gunn
Shirmaine Jones
Natalie Wood
Tom Gunn
John Vaillant
Zoe Grams
Michael Harris
Charles Montgomery
Kurt Wong
Lisa Bodhransong
Jacqueline Moore
Janet Fretter
Daniel Carroll
Sheena Starky
Brian Fearncombe
Howard Bobry
Nicole van de Leuv
Allison Bailey
Lorene Oikawa
Trina Ng
Bruce Weir

FAR FROM HOME

HOME

Essays Beyond the Comfort Zone

Edited by Tyee Bridge
Essays by J.B. MacKinnon, Susan Olding, Jake MacDonald,
Deborah Campbell, Scott Russell Sanders

N

www.nonvella.com

"Driving to This Point in History," © 2000 by J.B. MacKinnon. Reprinted
by permission. (Now titled "The Road Trip")

"Into the Lair of the White Bear," © 2008, by Deborah
Campbell. Reprinted by permission.

"The Commissioner" excerpted from With The Boys by Jake
MacDonald. Copyright 2005, Jake MacDonald. Reprinted by
permission.

"Such Good Girls" excerpted from Pathologies: A Life in Essays by Susan
Olding. Copyright 2008, Susan Olding. Reprinted by permission.

"Staying Put," © 1992, by Scott Russell Sanders. Reprinted by permission.
(Now titled "Settling Down")

MacKinnon, J. B. (James Bernard), 1970-, author

Far from home : essays beyond the comfort zone / edited by Tyee Bridge
; essays by J.B. MacKinnon, Susan Olding, Jake MacDonald, Deborah
Campbell, Scott Russell Sanders.

Issued in print and electronic formats.
ISBN 978-0-9936216-1-1 (pbk.)—ISBN 978-0-9936216-4-2 (epub)

1. Canadian essays (English)—21st century. I. MacDonald, Jake, 1949-,
author II. Sanders, Scott R. (Scott Russell), 1945- author III. Campbell,
Deborah, 1970-, author IV. Olding, Susan, author V. Bridge, Tyee, 1970-,
editor VI. Title.

PS8373.1.M32 2014   C814'.608   C2014-906065-3
                                     C2014-906066-1

CONTENTS

INTRODUCTION

HOME IS A narrow idea for most North Americans. It's usually applied to that private space where we live with (or without) our families—where we eat our toast, sleep our 6.7 hours (the high end of the national average), raise our children, watch television and do all the things our non-work hours allow us to do.

The idea of home encompasses wetlands and farmlands, backwoods and back alleys, and involves relationships not just with our families but with wolves, pizza chefs and entire landscapes. It can also be the place we return to remember something—or to atone for it, as in the classic line from Nikos Kazantzakis's *The Last Temptation of Christ*: "Thank you Lord, for bringing me where I did not want to come."

We've all felt far from home. It's a permanent feeling for some of us, where certain constants—people or places loved, even things as seemingly dependable as the seasons or unscheduled time—is long gone.

All of the authors in *Far From Home* hint at how, or how not, to find our place. J.B. MacKinnon (on a booze-fueled, satiric road trip to Reno) and Scott Russell Sanders (pondering the deep-rooted stubbornness of tornado-harried Midwesterners) both take some shrewd jabs at our inherited North American ideas about the open road and the romance of moving on. Susan

Olding, as coach of a high-school cheerleading squad, finds herself dealing with the scars of adolescence, that period when we first feel home slipping away. Jake MacDonald recalls hip-wader memories of region and family in his memoir of duck hunting with his father. And Deborah Campbell seeks out the white Kermode, or "spirit" bear—considered a relative by the Kitasoo/ Xai'xais peoples she visits in Klemtu—in a part of her coastal backyard she's never seen before.

Wendell Berry once referred to certain corporate employees as "itinerant professional vandals"—people without a stake in a place who can pillage it and move on. This is not called vandalism, he noted, because of its vast scale and profitability. Perhaps in our keep-on-truckin' culture we tolerate it because we've forgotten something important about where we live.

Our thanks go out to all the authors herein for pointing the way—and for their generosity in letting us republish these pieces. In the spirit of off-duty soul-searching, as well as rollicking good writing, it's an honor to present them to you.

TYEE BRIDGE, EDITOR

THE ROAD TRIP

J.B. MacKinnon

MY HOUNDSTOOTH SHIRT was badly torn and stuffed in a hotel ice bucket. The trapeze artist stared down from his queen-size to where I lay on the floor. The car keys were gone, my pockets empty. The whole scene raised pointed questions, a tale of decadence and human wreckage.

All I can say for now is, this is how things looked when I woke up in Reno.

"I HAVE A few errands to run across North America," I told the rental agent. I did not use the words "road trip."

"The car is America and America is the car," wrote Lydia Simmons, among others. "The car is the myth and metaphor for America," and the heart of the myth is the road trip. It is the image that gets those Xterras and Jettas off the lot, that moves those Acura Vigors and Chrysler 300Ms. Cars that drive the gridlock-to-soccer-camp Errandsville rut are sold with a serving of speed, open highway and reckless insanity, but you do not wave this road-trip platter under a rental agent's nose. He will suddenly picture you in a red convertible, the wind tootling across the mouth of your empty beer bottle ... put the hammer down through another corner ... twenty-seven miles to Happy Camp, California ...

There will be problems with your credit card.

The rental agent didn't need to know. Along with a photographer known all his adult life as Satan, I had official sanction to Cut Loose, and even close friends were seething with envy. For me, *the road*; for them, another week in their cubicles, craving escape from the urban purgatory. "Freedom is only for the strong!" I shouted through the driver's side window, then hit the four-way power locks and cranked the A/C. We pointed our silver nose south and shifted to D4. Romance and Adventure clung to us like leeches.

A road trip begins and ends with an automobile. Ours was a 1999 value-model Honda Civic sedan in Vogue Silver Metallic. At just over fourteen feet long, you can snap this sleek four-door through a 32.8-foot-diameter donut with one hand and with the other dial the cell to report yourself to the fun police. The aluminum-alloy in-line four-cylinder engine is a bit sleepy, kicking in just 106 horsepower at 6,200 rpm. On the flats we took the four-speed automatic front-wheel drive to a straining 111.6 mph—which will get you home from the in-laws' in an air-conditioned hurry—but we struggled on long grades and hills upward of eight percent.

Not all the numbers are so conservative, however. With a factory-spec estimate of 35 miles to the gallon over the 3,291 miles we rode this silver rocket, our stylish sedan let loose hundreds of pounds of carbon dioxide and monoxide, along with smog-forming hydrocarbons and nitrogen oxides. That's the world-shaking kick-ass power of multiport fuel injection.

Ten hours later the wind was tootling across my empty beer bottle and we put the hammer down through another corner. Everything felt right. We were with The People, throbbing along with the 24/7 economy. Driver's euphoria had struck just two hours into the trip: I was watching a trucker punch himself in the cheekbones to stay awake in the Seattle merge lane when suddenly 200 yards of open blacktop appeared in front of me and I answered with the throttle. "Ah, *freedom!*" I shouted. Satan was aiming his Brezhnev-era black Kiev camera at anyone with an "I love my country, but I fear my government" bumper sticker. We could taste the surging power of immediate off-ramp access to burritos, Adidas, beer, Ralph Lauren, drive-thru banking, Wal-Mart, aromatherapy.

We switched drivers beyond Oregon's northern border, where whirlwinds were sprouting from the Oak Creek valley topsoil. I flipped through my driver behavior notes. Dr. Paul Rau of the National Highway Traffic Safety Administration had explained one current theory—that long-distance drivers sink into a primitive vision system that corrects only for "fight or flight" responses. At 90 mph, of course, those responses are almost constant, a St. Vitus dance of short muscle fiber. All is observed but almost nothing absorbed. "Television mode," said Dr. Rau.

A dust devil reared up at the road's edge and streaked skyward into the I-5 haze.

"You're kind of driving on your brainstem," the doctor had said. "There's a disconnect. You get people who go into a situation and just watch it happen."

Out my window the dust devil had doubled in size and was keeping pace, marching along the roadbed like a 200-foot messiah. I stared blandly into the violence. Satan didn't seem to have noticed.

"Twister," I said finally, jerking my thumb at the maelstrom.

"Hm," he replied.

Honda insists this particular car has 'up-for-anything' attitude," and with fifty inches of hip room in the driver's seat, there's plenty of space for a bourbon bottle or martini shaker to help you get as "responsive, uninhibited" as the car itself. Don't worry: the Civic handles with the hair-on-fire rage of a Pamplona bull, the double wishbone suspension sucking it up through the tightest chute-the-chutes, the all-seasons finally squealing in the passing lane of an uphill hairpin at double the posted 25 mph limit. As your dealer—that's your Honda dealer—will tell you, "There's a time to be spontaneous. A time for opportunities, adventure..."

Esquire reports that the charmingly plain-jane Civic is fast becoming a customizer's favorite. Don't kid yourself that looks don't matter: if you're like most of us, your car will spend ninety percent of its "life" empty and parked. And don't worry about that sissy engine—remember that to haul your typical 150- to 200-pound body to work and back, you're relying on 2,388 pounds of plastic, aluminum and steel. Experts have compared this ratio to "a chainsaw cutting butter," and, if so, who cares if the blade is five feet long or six?

In Grants Pass, near the California border, we stopped for gas and to test our legs, wavering like newborn fawns. The air was impossibly still—it seemed to crackle with a sort of static force, which in fact was the explosive spattering of deep blue birdshit on the pavement. Thousands of starlings were gathering to scream into the twilight from three thin cedars at the station lot's edge. "It's like something from Children of the Corn!" shouted a man hunched over his crippled engine. We nodded, unnerved.

There is a catch-22 with driving: you should not drive while your judgment is impaired, yet long-distance driving is believed to impair judgment. Your heart rate, blood pressure and stress hormones hike up and stay up. We decided to take the edge off with a beer, and rolled down the windows to smell the sweet sweat of 1,000-year-old trees. In the dark, the redwoods' pinstriped trunks bellied right to the road, and you could imagine an ancient forest that stretched on forever. Neon COCKTAILS signs buzzed in the woods like will-o'-the-wisps. We were in the groove, riding high in the corners just to feel the G-forces in our eyeballs. The euphoria was peaking, and then we hit the California border roadblock.

The guard was approaching from some 100 yards off, but Satan was already hanging well out the window, waving one long arm like a dismissive exorcist. "We don't have a stitch of fruit or food or anything!" he shrieked. It sounded ridiculously suspicious—"Cocaine? None of that around here, my good man!"—but the official was focused on the reassuring lines of our '99 sedan. These are good people, the guard's eyes said, people who know the drill. "Well then, boys, you'd better get going," he said warmly. "Welcome to California."

We accelerated into the night, empties clinking in the back seat. "Release the fruit flies!" Satan cackled. I winced, peering into the trees for parabolic microphones. The border guard cares about one thing only: insect pestilence. All day, cars and trucks wheeze over the frontier, leaking oil and medical waste, delivering smuggled CFCs or the frozen makings of McDonald's Big Macs, no questions asked. But joke about fruit flies or apple maggots and you'll soon be dressed in a bright orange jumpsuit, picking up garbage on the Mexican border.

We had driven too long; sensation was dying. It was impossible to gauge the temperature of the air and the stars were a visual aggravation piercing down through the windshield. The beer tasted like dead cells. We hurtled along a Pacific shore cliff, hardly noticing as the stomach dropped out of the road and we suddenly roared out of the forest at sea level and straight into a convoy of parked mobile homes, stretching for miles beneath a waxing moon. Salt spray drifted past, distorting the halogen reflections of the RVs' great white panels. We felt in our marrow that these were serious Freedom Kampers, fellow travelers with Truths to Tell, and we resolved to return at dawn.

Near midnight, we stopped in Arcata, California, perhaps the most environmentally friendly town in North America. Sea breezes rushed through the parking lots of the franchise strip mall, and signs encouraged us not to dump paint thinner into the storm drains. I hefted a Motel 6 ledger like a Cro-Magnon testing a spearhead. We had seized freedom by the short and curlies. We toasted Romance and Adventure with another beer, and turned on the TV.

A THICK FOG was just lifting as we made our way back to the mobile home convoy. It was a new day, but in the flat light the RVs loomed huge overhead like ghost ships. They were bumper to bumper, a wall between the highway and a beach that was empty but for one man, his tiny shih tzu struggling in a vicious undertow. The morning traffic had already drowned the sound of the surf.

The first Freedom Kampers were just emerging. They had the weathered look of road gurus, unsnapping lawn furniture to spend another day watching the big trucks blast by on Route 101. They kept their backs to the sea, where a bleached sun breathed whirligigs into the mist. Finally, one broke rank to chop firewood from the shore, and I made my cautious approach. He turned and smiled, but kept a ready grip on the ax. I asked about the fishing.

"No fish left," he said. He had the pursed lips of a brontosaurus. "Ten years ago, you could catch dinner with an hour's casting in the surf. Nowadays..." He pointed into the fog to where trawlers ran the coast, taking every fish of marketable size. The story was the same on shore, he added. There are no golden bears left in the Golden Bear State, and the last of the elk needed strict protection. "Give them a day and they'd shoot every last one," the woodcutter said. These were dead forests and a dead sea.

I kicked the sand. Is *anything* left? "Mountain lion," he replied. Protests had shut down the cougar hunt, and now the hills were crawling with hungry cats. "Those damn environmentalists, they'll take everything right to the wall," the camper said, squinting into my eyes for any glimmer of tree-hugger sympathy. I had the eyes of a dead soul. He seemed pleased.

If the campers knew Truths, no one was talking. They were a suspicious clan, old men and women glaring out at paradise from inside ticky-tacky boxes. They were the circled chuckwagons of the pioneers, the gated communities of Des Moines and Tampa and Palm Springs. We had breached their defenses in a foreign-model car, and they sized us up for fags and liberals.

Which was just fine back in Arcata, where a drug trafficker was admiring our ride. "A '99 model?" We were obviously professionals, people with clout. "I've got some cool piercings," he said. "Would that be good for your magazine?" We were in a back alley, sampling Humboldt County's famous produce. It hit from below, a kneecapping drug that plunged upward through the viscera and rushed as a celestial river out the top of the skull. Satan started shooting the silver flashes of tongue and nipple. We were dealing with the final studs and rings when the cop appeared at our shoulders. "What's going on here?"

Eight bloodshot eyes swiveled toward him, pupils trembling with the nervousness of the busted. We clawed our way back to the bubble of reality and seized control. "We're professional journalists," Satan declared. "This young man had some intimate piercings, and we needed a private place for a photo-shoot."

"We'll be done in *precisely* five minutes," I added.
The officer surveyed the scene. Cameras. The smell of skunk. One well-pierced kid scrambling to put away his plumbing. No blood, no questionable political pamphlets, no illegal immigrants. Just a bunch of regular folks getting cranked up and taking obscene photographs. Why get involved? "This is private property," he said finally. "Finish up and then you'd better get going."

We crept back to Arcata's main square, drug-paranoid and buzzing from our brush with the law. The locals continued to hacky-sack, barter and drive electric cars. Bicycles wheeled by; a kid with acid-drop eyes played balance beam on the roof of a house. There was the look of freedom, but the pace was all wrong, everything so slow and public… Troopers rolled past, staring out at the job security of an endless stream of hopheads.

Elsewhere in America, men in suits drank shooters of human blood and cheered the Dow towards 15,000, and here the cops watched as people planted organic eggplant and organized public transit. Arcata was a pestilence to be contained, a grub in the apple. It was the ugly specter of horror-show birds descending on a lonely gas station. We got back in the car and ran the midnight mountains to Reno.

ALL ROADS LEAD to Reno. Along the way, billboards on towering pedestals sell you tires and pork ribs and Jesus. Our value Civic came with only the stock AM/FM 4X20 watt radio, but we could still spin that AM talk radio dial. "Does *your* candidate support federal grants for *dubious* art?"…"you need The Fat-Whacker!™"…"the Caligula-like atmosphere of the Clinton White House…"

You wonder. Are they really sleeping with their sisters out in Washington DC? Appointing horses to the Senate? Have they reinstated torture? Then you crest a hill and the town is there below you like a road-killed circus monkey, gaudy and crawling with maggoty movement. Freeways twist pointlessly in the desert; tall glittering buildings turn out to be parkades. Reno is the city where the losers finally won.

We met immediately with the trapeze artist, a Canadian with a flight to catch and a last-minute to-do list of sunken bars, hot tubs and sex shops. It sounded sensible—we had been driving for three days, and any moment of stillness triggered headaches and delirium tremens. We needed jolts and booze, and we found them at Shea's Tavern.

"I requested some country and western music," a wiry drunk said firmly as we settled in our stools.

"AND I TOLD YOU WE DON'T PLAY ANY FUCKING COUNTRY WESTERN MUSIC!" the bartender replied.

I leaned toward Satan: "This town makes me edgy." A local tipped his cap at us and cleared out. The aging hippie at one end of the bar was watching everyone's hands for sudden movements.

"GET THE FUCK OUT!" The bartender was screaming now, his triceps pulsing as he herded the drunk and his silent, dangerous-looking partner toward the door. Everyone stared into a beer or into space.

"Edgy," I repeated firmly.

"COME AND TRY IT, YOU FUCKING DRUNK!" the bartender screamed down the street as the winos cursed and threatened. He walked back in, sweat pouring off his shaved head. "What can I get you gentlemen?"

We drank and made small talk. The bartender was a former addict and Metallica roadie. The aging hippie was a specialist in local drug culture. The fat man at the end of the bar was mourning the recent closure of the Mustang Ranch bordello. Good people. Reno's people. The drunks would be back, the bartender said, tomorrow maybe. All they needed was a fistful of dollars. This is a nation that forgives anyone who refuses to change.

About half of all urban space in the U.S. is given over to automotive transport, so your vehicle is both a private "carcoon" and your place on the public stage. Honda knows the Civic has to reflect your "life-starts-at-midnight" streak and the caring side that tucks in the kids. Consider the energy put into the catalytic converter alone: as these anti-pollution devices became popular in the early '90s, an estimated six million tons of ore had to be refined for platinum each year. It takes a staggering amount of energy, fossil fuels and water to keep America driving, whether in an Edsel or an electric hybrid. The tires alone might contain Alabama steel, Indonesian pulpwood, Mexican oil and Louisiana sulfur, much of which gets "recycled" in tire fires or the hundreds of thousands of tons of rubber dust that wash off the nation's roads each year. Making a car is a global adventure, and it's up to you to take yours to the natural limits.

But what's this little sticker? "Auto pollution can promote or cause lung cancer, emphysema, respiratory infection, coronary heart disease, stress, low birth weight and immune system depression"? Just kidding folks—the politically correct crowd is still eating the auto industry's exhaust. As one British toxicologist said, "I won't smoke, if you don't drive." Pass that man an ashtray!

We moved on. In our carcoon we surfed the bandwidths from the heart of the Mojave Desert. "Americans are a head taller than one generation ago"... "Doctors expect Ms. Taylor to make a full recovery"..."the press themselves, probably, connected to the drug trade"..."maybe we should start voting with a bullet."

We could even tune in to talk-radio hero Art Bell, shouting

out from New Mexico about a torrent of UFO sightings, another season of record-strength hurricanes, fifty new "dead zones" in the world's oceans, whale corpses washing up on the West Coast, ecological chaos, worldwide extinctions, rain that leaves children vomiting and gasping for air...

But you're *driving*, friends, and you don't want a bummer like that on the dial. Just tap the search button and hit a new frequency... "The FatWhacker!™"... "there's no time left for losers"... "The Truth Will Set You Free!"

"DON'T TELL ME you saw the bats."

Mike the Vietnam vet is leaning down the bar toward where my eyes have settled on the poster for the seventeenth annual Testicle Festival. "You'll have a ball!" it promises, but Mike is demanding my attention. "The bats," he says again, turning heads in Strozzi's Bar.

You have heard, surely, of the great bats of the Nevada high desert, as featured in Hunter S. Thompson's *Fear and Loathing in Las Vegas*. You assumed they were hallucinations, but the bats are very real.

The first one wheeled out of the sky at twilight on Route 50, "the Loneliest Road in America." It turned one gold blind eye into the headlights, kissed a moth out of the air inches from the windshield, then swept overhead like the Angel of Death. Its body was the size of a Florida grapefruit.

The bats had made an impression on Mike. It had disturbed him when he drove his '77 Volkswagen van into a plague of locusts and saw enormous shadows twisting through the crossfire. He was even more uncomfortable to know the shadows had been real.

Mike is taking us back, back along the escape route from Reno, across Nevada to Utah and north to the southernmost slip of Montana. He is a gentle soul, his face lined with equal parts anxiety and kindness. After years in Washington, he realized he had "no real attachments" and went out to look for some. "It took me forty-seven years to figure out that I'm a hippie," he says.

He spent much of his life as a military man, and now conformity and regimentation open dark chambers in his mind. Mike can't drive the 41,000 miles of interstate highway knowing that Eisenhower took their inspiration from the Nazi autobahns. The interstates were launched in 1956 as a project to allow total mobility of American troops on their own soil, and were cheered by the auto makers and corporate truckers. Today the freeways are crowded, *worshipped*, by paranoids who believe black government helicopters are preparing the nation for global martial law.

Mike sticks to the byways, the old auto-camping routes—"Thoreau at 29 cents a gallon"—where America broke away from the punch-clock orthodoxy of the locomotive. Mike went looking for that lost tribe of freedom fighters, and found a nation of gas station hawkers and roadside mini-golf. Worse, he found himself: a "character" in a roadside bar, an "experience" for fellow travelers in the economy of perpetual escape.

Except, perhaps, on Route 50 through eastern Nevada, the bedrock of the old Pony Express, our escape route out of Reno. The night before we fled, we had celebrated America. We had cheered its economy in a million slot machines, its future in all-you-can-eat buffets where no one speaks and the ceiling is painted to look like a spring sky.

Grandmothers dressed as leprechauns had urged us to gamble and get drunk, and on-duty police officers had directed us to a nightclub featuring perfect women with flesh-colored surgical bandages on their breasts. Any man with a dollar in his teeth could have those breasts pressed in his face, and a $20 bill would buy a lap dance and souvenir calendar. Drinks flowed, sex and booze and high style, and for the right price everything was for sale, even a pair of leopard-print French heels straight off the feet of a twenty-year-old dancer named Jillicious, from Orlando. Black valets handed out cigars in the washroom, Saudi princes slapped high-fives with freshmen from Iowa and out on the streets they were locking up the Circus Circus fun-house but the gamblers played on, sinking nickels for a chance at a candy-apple red convertible Mustang rotating overhead on a fifteen-foot pedestal.

At the end of the night I lay on my back at the base of a fiber-glass cliff, staring up past the fiberglass pines into the eyes of a giant ram, his goat-face framed by curling horns. Perfume from the leopard-print shoes wafted over my face. The whole scene was lit in forest green light, then amber, and finally red. I was faintly aware that all of this was in the middle of a giant parking lot, but my thoughts were on Caligula. What is it that the devi-ant Roman says in Albert Camus' play? Something about "the stale smell of pleasure"?

And then I woke up on the hotel room floor with the car keys lost and my pockets cleaned out and a pair of round punc-tures on my belly. That's the Law of the Fang, buddy. That's the freedom of the road.

THERE WERE THE predictable hassles getting out of Reno, but then—suddenly, finally—we were on Route 50. There was no traffic, no towns, nothing for sale. Just mountain ridges and great blue valleys, prisons and abandoned dune buggies. War planes turned tricks in the sky. It was along this road that a man with a U.S. Forest Service permit cut down "Prometheus," a 4,950-year-old bristlecone pine that turned out to have been the oldest living thing on Earth.

Route 50 is it. The drive parches your mind and crushes you with its loneliness, and then darkness hits and you soar dead-eyed into a maze of life: bored and jaded jackrabbits diving at the wheels, snakes and mice and bats, the ghostly white asses of pronghorn antelope, the key-lime eyes of coyotes, and always, always the King Kong drumming of locusts on the windshield. For a horrible moment you imagine a dying wheeze from the engine, the stunning silence of automotive breakdown on a moonlit byway. Nothingness. And then, out of the placeless total darkness, a line of, is it torches? Torches on the horizon, and beneath them now you see a clutch of pale faces, queer strangers marching towards you achingly slow…

We made Utah and the moon shone clear light over the seismic faults.

Give it back, I thought. We have escaped and found freedom and under no circumstances are we stopping the car. *Give it back. Roll up this road to nowhere and give the Great Empty back to the creatures of the night.*

MY BODY IS eating itself. Satan tosses and turns and gibbers in his sleep. Each day we get up earlier and pick ever more distant points on the map. Today, non-stop to the end of the line. "It should be no trouble," I say. "We don't seem to need to eat anymore." We take Route 191 toward the I-90. The car smells like a hunger striker's cell. Small cuts have ceased to heal. My eyes tremble in their sockets.

The highways of Montana run the courses of rivers and are lined with white crosses. Each crucifix, most marked with a tiny Stars and Stripes, represents a person killed in a crash. We have packed survivalist Robert Young Pelton's Come Back Alive, which features a quiz.

The most likely cause of accidental death for hikers in the U.S. is (dying in a car accident).

The most dangerous job in America is (truck driver).

The most dangerous activity in America is (driving).

I imagine the bodies all planted together in a single cemetery. Forty thousand new corpses a year, and three million disfigured wounded to limp around visiting the dead. A special section for two- to twenty-four-year-olds, for whom car crashes are by far the leading cause of death. What a roadside attraction it would be, well worth driving off the interstate to check out, maybe buy a t-shirt, have a coffee at the Roadkill Cafe. Montana could use a tourist magnet like that.

For ten hours, I refuse to surrender the wheel. Another day of Taco Time, a Super 8 day of Comfort Inn, 7-11, Denny's, the temporary discomfort of BP Gas. Another 500 miles of déjà vu. And now home is minutes away. A full moon, fat and blood red, is squeezed between the smog belt and a whip of cloud, suspended for the moment between roadside signs for Chevron and Travelodge.

I write a final note: "That red moon. Beautiful. But what does it advertise? Dubious art?"

I remember a promise to myself made before I hit the road: swim. I would not let a swimming hole pass by, not stew in my own sweat with a lake or green river ready to carry my naked body to the cool roots of time. But for seven days of summer heat, I let those lakes and rivers fly by.

And now I remember "Followers" and its poet Jim Harrison:

...we think a man can dive
in a pond, swim across it,
and climb a tree though few of us do.

This trip is over.

INTO THE LAIR OF THE WHITE BEAR

Deborah Campbell

MIST HANGS OVER moss-shrouded old growth where eagles perch, their enormous nests strewn with bones like ogres' dens. Shiny harbor seals bob up from the water, staring curiously at us, their faces like Labrador pups. Dead salmon, having recently spawned, are draped over rocks like silver stoles, slung from river-nudging branches like laundry or floating belly-up downstream, their mission accomplished.

"Sex and death," says the first mate on the *Maple Leaf*, the ninety-two-foot schooner that has taken me and eight other passengers on a nine-day journey into one of the last great wildernesses, a remote expanse of British Columbia coastline that stretches all the way to Alaska. "Better than HBO."

It is spawning season in the Great Bear Rainforest, an archipelago of thousands of islands and webbed fiords roughly the size of Lake Ontario. Known (in the poetry of industrial discourse) as the Mid-Coast Timber Supply Area until environmentalists brought it to international attention in the 1990s, the Great Bear is one of the world's largest intact coastal temperate rain forests. It's one of the last inhabitable regions of the planet that, on satellite images, still turns black at night.

Our journey had begun in the coastal First Nations fishing village of Bella Bella. The sun had just broken through the roiling clouds when Kevin Smith, the red-bearded owner of Maple Leaf Adventures and captain of the *Maple Leaf*—British Columbia's oldest tall ship—greeted us on the dock. The Gore-Tex-clad passengers who clambered up and over the mahogany railing were all adventurous professionals, Canadian and American, nearly unanimous in their mission: to glimpse the most famous resident of this rain forest—the white kermode, or spirit bear. "It's the rarest bear on the planet," said Smith, a former park ranger and geographer—rarer than China's panda bears. And it's famously elusive.

Striking out into the wilderness, I inhaled air filtered by millions of conifers—1,000-year-old red cedar, western hemlock, Sitka spruce. A humpback whale raced along the coastline, thumping its enormous tail. Four caramel-colored sea lions cavorted in the waters near shore. That night, a storm hit, lashing our vessel. Secure in my bunk in the wheelhouse, I dreamt of looking for a place I could not find. As dawn forced its way through the morning mist, I awoke to discover that we had anchored in a protected bay next to the rusted hull of a century-old shipwreck. A reminder that for every island we pass, more lurk just below the surface.

AFTER BREAKFAST, PRIMED with steaming mugs of fair-trade organic coffee, we board two inflatable Zodiacs and zip into Mussel Inlet, where we immediately see signs of what our onboard naturalist, Alison Watt, calls the "divine, spectacularly mortal salmon," a line from Canadian poet Don McKay. In Bella Bella, the fishing boats sit idle, hard hit by the decline in salmon stocks. Out here, where the unruly Pacific laps up against the mouths of rivers, some of these spectacularly mortal beings still live out their primordial drama, growing snouts and fangs in a Jekyll-to-Hyde transformation as they fight their way to a redemptive death.

This place, explains Watt, should really be called the Great Salmon Rainforest. Salmon are the foundational species that supports bears, wolves, minks, eagles, ravens, all the way down to what she calls the "non-charismatic microfauna," a sly comment that exposes how obsessed we humans are with the big and beautiful animals when the tiny and ignored are just as essential. None matter more, though, than the salmon that have journeyed to spawn and then die in the rivers where they were born. Carried deep into the woods by all manner of creatures, their bodies fertilize the soil with nitrogen, creating growth bursts in trees, which in turn protect the rivers and the salmon from runoff.

One snouted beast on the river's edge has had his juicy eye plucked out by an eagle or a raven or one of the thousands of dovelike mew gulls that breed in Alaska and pause here on their migration south. Others, half gutted, indicate the presence of bears.

As we trudge through the sedges in rain gear, a black grizzly rears up from the shoreline, its cavernous mouth chewing silverweed root, its back a great muscular hump. A ways off, a tawny-colored grizzly mother and her nearly weaned cub are sharing a salmon.

As wilderness disappears, so do the grizzlies, but that is not the only risk to their survival. In a month or two, says our captain, bear viewing will turn to the licensed bear hunt. This grizzly mother and cub, part of a declining population that has already disappeared from ninety-nine percent of its habitat in the United States and most of southern British Columbia, will be seen through a rifle scope rather than a camera lens.

For now, they barrel awkwardly into the water for a fresh catch.

THERE ARE SALMON enough for us too: wild coho, line-caught in these waters, prepared by our excellent chef. At night, we dine below deck, wedged around a mahogany table, sharing Okanagan pinot blanc, organic Argentine red and any words we know for rain. Books on seafaring, First Nations mythology and the region's flora and fauna fill the built-in shelves around us. Above, a skylight opens onto the deck.

Our conversations drift invariably toward the world's problems, issues forced upon us by the immediacy of a wilderness that has become, to most of humanity, something ancient, mythic, falling away, recalled mainly through the prism of Saturday-afternoon nature documentaries (Japanese and BBC film crews are in the area). Sandy, an epidemiologist and amateur photographer from Toronto, decided to take her vacation in the rain forest because of a "fear that this is disappearing." Though I grew up next to the second- and third-growth woodlands of southern British Columbia, I was unaware that there are still places like this, where hundreds of dolphins race our ship over the course of half an hour one morning, leaping and diving like synchronized swimmers. It occurs to me that I have become an urbanite, as transformed in my vision of the world as the world itself has been transformed by my culture's vision for it.

WE ARE ABOUT as far off the grid as is possible in the modern world. Our only bathing takes place at natural hot springs, our only communication is with the creatures we encounter, and every attempt is made to minimize our impact on a place threatened from all sides by the reality from which we've come: logging, mining, big-game sport hunting, salmon farming and mounting pressure to permit oil and gas exploration, as well as rising tanker traffic as the North melts. Even with a groundbreaking 2006 agreement between conservation groups, industry, First Nations, local communities and government, less than thirty percent of the Great Bear Rainforest is protected, and even that is open to hunting. This is naturalist Watt's fourth trip to the rain forest, and she has yet to see a spirit bear. Even if we don't, she has already begun to chronicle some of the dozens of other species we see on our excursions into one of the most biologically productive forests left on earth. In a mist-covered estuary one morning, we count one hundred eagles perched like sentinels on the tops of ancient trees. Rounding a bend in the river, we come upon a lone white swan. That afternoon, two Dall's porpoises—the world's second fastest-swimming mammal (after the blue whale)—chase the ship below my perch on the bowsprit. Reaching down, I can almost touch their silvery skin.

MARVIN ROBINSON, A thirty-nine-year-old Gitga'at from Hartley Bay, is the resident "bear guy" on Gribble Island, his band's ancestral territory and one of the only places in the world where spirit bears are found. Originally thought to be albinos, these bears are the product of a double recessive gene, such that local black bears, on occasion, produce startlingly white cubs.

Standing in waterproof rain pants and a baseball cap to address us, Robinson explains the bear-viewing rules. "Stay in a group. Don't run. Your instincts trigger the bears," he warns, solemnly scanning the group, "to hunt you." Point taken.

Walking single file through a forest of alders, we arrive at the creek where the Gitga'at have built viewing platforms designed to safeguard bear feeding patterns. Dozens of pink salmon are jostling one another on their way upstream. "It's been ten years since they logged this island," says Robinson, "and the salmon are just starting to come back." A ferret-like pine marten tugs a salmon its own size into the woods, while another steals up a dead tree to raid a bird nest.

A black bear emerges from the forest and ambles down to the creek. Pausing to fix us with a glance, it paws up a salmon.

We sit, cameras ready, watching and being watched. Suddenly, another bear appears from the brush a hundred yards downstream.

Looking like a polar bear that has taken a wrong turn south, the spirit bear wades into the creek. I look at Jo, a veteran police officer from Ottawa. She has tears in her eyes.

The bear pauses to sniff the air. "He smells some hairless twolegs," whispers Captain Smith.

FOR THE NEXT hour, the world's rarest bear sorts through the salmon buffet spread upon the creekside, in search of caviar, casually ducking its head beneath the waters to better see the parade yet to spawn.

Back at his boat, Robinson describes the many threats to the spirit bear's survival. Though it's illegal to hunt the white bear, it's perfectly legal to hunt its sisters and brothers, and "any black bear shot on this island is probably taking a recessive gene for a white bear." Rumors have been circulating that a kermode was shot. If so, Robinson thinks a suitable punishment can be found in the ancient aboriginal tradition of burying a slave in the ground beneath a new totem pole. As he speaks, a barge carrying a forest's worth of logs passes through the waters behind him.

The First Nations village of Klemtu was a fishing community until the salmon downturn several years ago. There, we meet Francis Robinson, a seventy-year-old elder of the four hundred Kitasoo/Xai'xais peoples who live in Klemtu (half of whom are Robinsons). Maple Leaf Adventures and a couple of other small-scale ecotour operators have signed protocol agreements with Klemtu, paying to be in its territorial waters (the funds sponsor a watchman program to halt bear poaching) and inviting the Kitasoo/Xai'xais to communicate and interpret their culture to guests. It's part of a drive to change the local economy from resource extraction to conservation while honoring local traditions.

At his village's stunning new cedar longhouse, its magnificent totem poles standing sentry, Robinson relates the story of the spirit bear. It was the raven who created the world, he says. When he created the bears, he made one in every ten white in order to remind the world of the ice age. Shortly after the longhouse was built in 2002, says Robinson, a spirit bear swam over to it. "Our chief was not surprised. He said it was just one of our relatives coming to visit."

Walking back to the *Maple Leaf*, accompanied by a stray dog that looks half wolf, we pass a boat delivering a load of farmed salmon to the Klemtu processing plant. The longhouse, the most spectacular in the Great Bear Rainforest, was financed by donations from fish farms and other organizations. "Human industry is the largest-scale experiment we've ever done," says Smith. "Protected areas are our only controls. They will be our blueprints for future generations to put the world back together again."

At the mouth of the river, I see a wild chum leaping high into the air.

THE COMMISSIONER

Jake MacDonald

I N THE TELEVISION series *Batman* there was a character known as Commissioner Gordon. I never understood what Commissioner Gordon did for a living, but my father had the same job. He was the commissioner of Metropolitan Winnipeg. When my friends asked me about his occupation, I said, "He's like Commissioner Gordon on *Batman*," and that seemed to satisfy them.

Unlike the silvery-haired buffoon on the TV show, my father was a stand-up guy, an unpretentious and popular boss who often wore his beat-up parka to the office and received friendly waves from janitors, street cops, firemen and other city employees wherever he went. He was the sort of guy they used to call a "Roosevelt liberal," a believer in good government and a champion of the underdog.

My father loved nature, especially birds. At our summer cottage on Lulu Lake, in northwestern Ontario, he put home-made birdhouses in each tree. On summer days the wooded yard was alive with a jazz festival of birds—redwings and warblers and jays and flycatchers and sparrows—darting through the foliage and filling the air with a wild partying chatter. My father's favorite birds were ducks and geese. He had paintings of exotic ducks on the cottage walls, and the bookshelf at home was filled with massive textbooks and coffee-table books about waterfowl.

He also loved hunting. Every fall, "Mac" (as my mother called him) went duck hunting for four or five weekends with his friends in the marshes of western Manitoba. Some people might find it hard to understand how a man who loved birds could also take pleasure in hunting them. My mother is the sort of person who will go to some lengths to capture a bumblebee in a jar rather than swat it with a newspaper, so I don't know what she thought of the bird-hunting issue. But she seemed to accept it, as part of his gruff outdoorsy style. My four sisters, although passionate animal lovers opposed to both guns and hunting, never indicated that they felt anything other than reverence for all his habits. Those were the days before one's automobile, hobbies and diet were considered statements, and I don't think it ever crossed my dad's mind that what he did in his spare time was anyone's damn business. He never explained why he hunted, or why he wanted me to hunt alongside him, but I think he had a notion that the rituals of the hunt would teach me something.

So every Thursday afternoon in October we'd load the big white 1959 Buick with wonderfully masculine stuff—sleeping bags, chest waders, boots, duck decoys, whisky, coolers stuffed with steaks, garlic sausage, stinky cheeses, and Black Label beer, guns, ammunition and, of course, my dad's huge World War II canvas navy bag, stuffed to bursting with heavy-duty clothes. We didn't take our golden retriever, Daisy, because she disapproved of firearms. She would prance around the car with her tail wagging until she saw the long sheepskin cases containing the shotguns, then drop her head and fold her tail between her legs and slink toward the house, opting to spend a weekend on the couch instead of coming out with the boys.

With the trunk and the back seat loaded, we'd head out into the countryside, which was never so beautiful as in autumn. By nightfall, we'd be bouncing along the mud road toward Marsh Manor, our hunting lodge, a decrepit, mouse-infested old City of Winnipeg trolley bus that my dad and his buddies had mounted, on blocks, next to a prairie marsh that the government map called Lake 15.

That night, while coyotes howled in the nearby woods and a huge harvest moon rose over the hill, they'd barbecue gigantic t-bone steaks slathered with onions. After dinner they'd play a few rounds of poker and drink a whisky or two before bed. My father's friends owned hunting dogs, but the dogs had proven themselves so citified that none were worth bringing on an actual hunting trip. I was therefore the honorary dog, and I would sit in the corner like a young Lab, wagging my tail when spoken to. There was a naughty calendar on the wall, or at least what passed for a naughty picture in those days—I think it involved a leggy redhead in gumboots and a pair of long johns—and they liked teasing me about it. "Son, you stick to the redheads and the canvasbacks, and we'll take care of the redheads and the blondes."

My dad had given me a heavy, flannel-lined arctic sleeping bag for my birthday, and I loved sleeping in it, pulling it over my head so the mice wouldn't run across my face. I'd climb into bed and fall asleep while the men were still playing cards, and then suddenly the alarm clock would be hammering. It would be five in the morning, and I'd jump out of bed because it was time to go hunting. The men, who took these trips not so much for the hunting as for the food, would of course begin the day by preparing another vast meal, this time bacon and eggs, with thick slabs of fresh bakery bread propped up on a wire toasting rack above the flaming hole in the old cast-iron wood stove.

When the toast was browned, my dad would slather on butter and strawberry jam and then stack the slabs in a tall column atop the stove, ready to be deployed when the tin plates were warmed and the bacon and eggs were ready. After breakfast, we dressed in several layers of heavy clothes and launched our canoes into the marsh.

As we dipped our paddles, skim ice bonked against the canvas hull of the canoe. There were millions of stars all around us. It was like canoeing through the sky, like being Wynken, Blynken and Nod, who paddled on a river of crystal light into a sea of dew. Invisible wings whistled past in the darkness. When we got to the grassy point where we would hunt, my dad would maneuver the canoe and I would drop the decoys in the water, making sure the anchor lines were untangled and the birds floated upright. Then we'd retire into the high cane grass along the shore and make ourselves a hiding place with a clear view of the decoys. Even on a cold morning it was cozy once you got tucked into the reeds, made yourself a padded seat with a burlap sack and unscrewed the lid of the Thermos to drink some of the steaming hot chocolate that my dad had prepared while the bacon was frying.

By now, the eastern sky would be streaked with pink, heating the air just enough to waken the breeze and set the cane grass swaying. Morning was coming, and with it came the exciting prospect of the appearance of the ducks. If an early mallard streaked through the sunrise, clawing overhead, my dad would stand up and point his gun. Bang! The gun would shoot flame, and even if he missed (Damn!), ducks being difficult to hit, I was pleased to watch the duck streak away and smell the delicious gunpowder on the morning air. Right now all my friends, poor saps, were trudging to school, and I felt extraordinarily lucky to be here.

During my first couple of years on the hunt, I wasn't allowed to shoot. My job was to run around in the bulrushes and look for downed birds. But finally, I got my chance. It was a beautiful sunny day, so lazy and warm that the duckies weren't flying. At eleven o'clock in the morning, my dad decided we'd give it another fifteen minutes, then head in. "Can I hold the gun?" I asked him. "And take a shot if a duck comes?"

No reasonable man would have enjoyed sharing a tippy canoe with a small boy armed with a large shotgun. But my dad liked giving people more credit than they probably deserved, and he handed me the gun. It was his Remington, a Model 870 Wingmaster. It was almost as long as I was, and I loved its impressive heft, its scarred woodwork and its sweet aroma of gun oil. A moment later, as if dispatched by God, a flying duck appeared out of nowhere, dodging through the cattails at high speed. I snapped off the safety, placed the front sight in front of the duck and pulled the trigger. The gun slammed me in the shoulder, making an enormous boom, and the duck crashed into the water. Oh my god, I thought. I've killed one.

We paddled out into the marsh. The duck was floating on the calm blue water. There wasn't a mark on the bird, and it was stone dead. My father didn't congratulate me or tell me I'd made a nice shot. He was the sort of man who didn't talk at moments like that. But I think I caught a trace of a private smile as he picked up the duck and handed it to me. It was a beautiful little blue-winged teal, limp, warm and radiantly feathered. I examined its lacquered bill and leathery feet, and later that day, in the front seat of the car, I held it in my hands all the way back to Winnipeg. For days, I kept the duck out in the garage and spent many hours visiting with it. The duck made a great temporary pet, albeit a dead one.

I was now washed in the blood, as they say, a certified duck hunter, and over the next few years my father taught me how to become a better one. He showed me how to set up decoys and blinds in a grain field so that waterfowl, as they circle endlessly, won't detect a trick. He taught me how to identify ducks at a distance, how to pluck them and clean them, and how to cook them for dinner. A fat mallard, stuffed with apples and roasted at 450 Fahrenheit, was in fact the first meal I ever cooked for myself.

But duck hunting wasn't simply about shooting ducks. It was about everyday life, and as always, my father wasn't inclined to make speeches about it. He tended to instruct by inference, allowing me to make my own decisions. If I screwed up, the only sign was a certain lack of feedback. By fine-tuning my powers of intuition, I began to realize that even if you're hungry, you probably shouldn't just open the fridge and stand there stuffing food in your mouth. You shouldn't offer your own fascinating opinion when other people are talking. You shouldn't claim you hit every duck that falls within eighty yards of your blind. And you shouldn't rehash a day's hunt by reminding everyone of what a good shot you were, especially if it's true.

My father and his friends came from a different generation. They didn't switch on automatic, hundred-watt smiles when posing for photographs. They didn't schmooze. And they didn't believe in lathering kids with compliments and "positive reinforcement." Today, not many kids use the prefix "Mister" when they are speaking to their father's friends. But even though I knew my father's friends very well, I would no sooner call them by their first names than I would snatch the cigar out of their mouths. Like my dad, they were lofty figures in my eyes, characters who belonged on Mount Rushmore. Because they were so reluctant to offer praise, I worked twice as hard to get it.

Eventually I grew up. I became a man myself, with a car

and a girlfriend and hunting buddies of my own, and I became uninterested in hunting with Mr. Caton and Mr. Bole and all the other demigods of my dad's acquaintance. They didn't seem to take it as seriously. They'd stand there drinking coffee while ducks flew right overhead. They would miss easy shots, over and over, and then joke about it. "How was your hunting trip?" I'd ask my dad when he got home.

"The weather was beautiful," he'd answer. "On Thursday afternoon there was a stunning migration of redtail hawks. Hundreds of them."

"How many ducks did you get?"

He'd shrug. "We got enough."

Sure, Dad. I'd gotten into the habit of evaluating a duck hunt by a single measure—body count. When the old guys blundered around in the marsh and came home almost empty-handed, talking about migrating hawks and beautiful weather, I knew they were putting on a brave face. They couldn't hunt very well anymore, and they didn't want to admit it.

One day my dad went up to Netley Marsh for a hunt with a few of his cronies, and while he was there, his friend Dick Bonnycastle died of a heart attack. I had to drive up and tell him Dick was gone. Dick was part of the original gang of elders. He was an ally of mine. He was a good shot, and he flew his own plane. He had also built one of the biggest publishing companies in the world, Harlequin Books. He'd died behind the controls of his Cessna, like the grand outdoorsman he was, and I hoped that if I ever got old, two or three centuries from now, I would make a similarly theatrical exit.

Pretty soon the other members of his group started appearing in the obituaries, one by one, and my dad's hunting trips became fewer and farther between. His old Remington pump hung untouched on its rack on the knotty pine wall of his rec room, and when I had a good hunt, I would take him a few mallards for his Sunday dinner. On his seventy-fifth birthday, I decided to take him out for a special treat, a first-class hunt. I would try to show him the sort of adventure that he'd shown me as a kid, and thereby thank him for introducing me to waterfowl hunting. The only question was, where would we go?

Marsh hunting was out of the question. Mud flats and tippy boats would be too much for a man of his age. Field shooting is always an uncertain proposition. At least half the time, field shoots end up a bust, and I was looking for a high-percentage opportunity. Luckily there was a slight shift in the migratory flyway that year, and eastern Manitoba began swarming with large flocks of geese. Forty miles east of Winnipeg an old hunting buddy of mine, Paul Craft, lives in a gorgeous log house next to a wooded creek. Paul agreed to do some scouting to line up a field for the three of us. A few nights later, the phone rang.

"Okay, we're in business," Paul announced, without identifying himself. "They're in the cornfield down the road."

"Canadas?"

"Both snows and Canadas, two or three thousand of them. They've been there a couple of days, and they're flying right in, acting like they own the field."

"Great. Count us in."

"Better be in the yard by six."

My dad was skeptical when I called and asked him if he wanted to go on a goose hunt the next morning. "I don't even have a hunting license."

I reminded him Canadian Tire was open until nine o'clock at night. He had plenty of time to pick up a license and some shells. "This is going to be a good shoot," I told him. "You don't want to miss this."

I could hear Dad chuckle. He'd been on plenty of wild goose

chases in his day, and he had a healthy skepticism about both the predictability of the birds and the dependability of his eldest son.

The next morning I got up at four-thirty. As I loaded the Jeep in the garage behind my house, I could hear the beagle yelp of migrating geese drifting down from skies high above the city. I drove over to my dad's, picked him up, and we headed out of town. Ah yes, the old feeling. The game was afoot. The Trans-Canada Highway was deserted, and the radio whispered with atmospheric skip, picking up wispy scraps of country music and talk shows from Kansas City or Chicago. They were the same talk shows with the same screwball callers that we had listened to on mornings like this many years ago. But now, I was driving and my dad was in the passenger seat. The tables were turned, but I could still feel the silent scrutiny of my driving ability every time I flicked on a turn signal and pulled out to pass a semi.

We arrived at Paul's forty minutes later. As we pulled into the driveway the lights were shining yellow in the kitchen and the eastern sky was turning pink. Coyotes were singing from the woods, and a group of Labrador pups rolled around on the deck. The whole scene looked like something out of an old L.L. Bean hunting calendar, except that when Paul came out he was wearing pressed slacks and a necktie. "Unexpected business complication," he said. "So I can't join you. But I set up the blind, and you guys can hunt the field on your own."

I think my father would have been just as happy to spend the morning doing odd jobs on Paul's property and horsing around with the Labrador pups. But the sky was lightening and I was keen to ambush some geese. Following Paul's truck out of the yard, we cruised along a grassy tractor trail, then out into a cornfield. Broken cornstalks rattled and thumped on the underside of the Jeep as we followed Paul to the center of the field, where a tall, odd-looking blind stood out like a phone booth. "What's this?" my father said.

I told him that Paul and I had started using this type of blind a few years ago. We hung a roll of chicken wire with cornstalks and staked it upright in the field, and the geese didn't seem to mind it a bit. Paul wished us luck and left for his meeting. We set up thirty-six decoys in a ragged V-shape upwind of the blind. Then we got settled in the blind, along with the two wooden crates that Paul had thoughtfully left for us as seats. My father was vastly amused by all of this, and I had to remind him to load his gun. "The geese could show up any minute," I said.

He chuckled again. He had good reason to question the odds of bagging a goose. When he was young, wild geese were rare on the Prairies, and nothing was more precious for Thanksgiving dinner than a big Canada goose. In the past four decades, since wetland conservation groups like Ducks Unlimited have established waterfowl refuges all up and down the Mississippi flyway, wild goose populations have exploded. In some places, there are so many that city people regard them as a nuisance, "rats with feathers." But waterfowl hunters continue to be reverential about geese, and I couldn't imagine a better birthday present for my father.

We sat in silence for the next ten minutes, watching the daylight gradually intensify the color of the russet cornfield. Coyotes were yipping along the river, and occasionally a flock of unseen ducks whispered overhead. I decided to give my dad first crack at any geese that came in. Don't outshoot him too badly, I lectured myself. Remember, it's his birthday.

Unlike ducks, geese usually wait until broad daylight before they start moving. The sun had no sooner started to spill over the horizon than I heard a distant yelp. A ragged line of pencil checks appeared above the treeline. "Here they come!" I hissed.

The geese crossed the line of trees on the eastern side of the field, then cupped their wings and glided toward us, leveling off only at the last moment to give our decoys a dutiful flyaround. Geese are usually cautious when they approach a field, and a bit of movement or even a glint of sunlight on a plastic decoy can scare them off. But Paul was right. These geese behaved as if they owned the field. After turning onto final approach, they dropped their gear and glided into the decoys.

Despite my promise to myself, when a large goose broke ranks and came gliding right over the blind, I couldn't resist raising my gun. I swung the front bead past the bird's cheek patch and jerked the trigger. Even as the gun went off I realized, with the twinge of self-loathing so familiar to the choke artist, that I'd not only broken my vow but missed the bird.

My father's Remington was now booming beside me. I twisted the gun upward and tried a second shot, focusing on a section of open sky about a yard ahead of my fleeing goose. This might have been a decent lead under normal circumstances, but since the goose was more or less stationary, clawing for altitude overhead, the shot charge had no more effect than to change the bird's expression from amazement to disgust. With an aggressive thrash of his wings he flew away.

My dad stepped out of the blind and walked toward two large geese that were lying on the stubble, stone dead.

So much for embarrassing him with my marksmanship. A few minutes later another flock appeared, snow geese this time, and my father once again shot a double. He made it look both awkward and graceful, clambering to his feet with some difficulty, settling the gun against his shoulder and crumpling first one goose, then another. I managed to tweak a bird myself this time, a juvenile goose that suddenly lost fire in one engine and crash-landed into the stubble. As soon as I picked it up, I heard a distant yelping and had to rush back to the blind. For the next hour that's how it went, one flock after another, with my father outshooting me on every pass. Then, after a ninth dead goose had been added to the pile at our feet, he shucked an empty cartridge out of his gun and announced, "Okay, that's enough."

"What do you mean? We haven't got our limit yet." I'd killed the last goose cleanly and was beginning to recover my groove. This was the end of a long bad-luck streak, and I wanted payback. I couldn't count the number of mornings I'd gone goose hunting and gotten skunked, lying in mud in the freezing rain while birds by the thousands settled into a field a mile away.

"We don't need a limit," he said, jacking the last shell out of his gun.

It was his birthday, so I couldn't argue the point. I didn't know it was his last hunt, but I suppose he did. Soon enough he would be crippled by a stroke, and the only geese he would see would be those flying high above the roof of his hospital. So he wanted to end his hunting career the way he had always lived it, as a man of fairness and moderation. He stepped out of the blind and walked toward a dead bird that was lying among the decoys, and then it happened.

A honk like the squeeze-horn of an old Ford Model "A" sounded in the distance and a very large, lone Canada goose came beating out of the sunrise. Standing at my dad's side, I watched the bird approach. I was pleased that I hadn't unloaded my gun. Solitary geese can be dumb at times. Although we were standing right in the open, the goose assumed the decoys were long-lost buddies and flew right toward us, honking plaintively.

"Should I shoot?"

My father didn't answer. In only a moment, the goose would cross the threshold into gun range. But time slowed down, and

I became sharply aware of the importance of this instant, the layering of memory, the many watercolor paintings I'd seen depicting this exact scene—this same sunrise, these same two hunters frozen in their tracks, and the silent figure of the older one, the father, standing there like a patient instructor, watching that last goose approach and refusing to answer his son's question.

Instead of lifting the gun and shooting at the goose, I lifted my arm and waved. The old goose flared in alarm, and we both stood there and watched it fly away.

SUCH GOOD GIRLS

Susan Olding

SURPLUS TO THE system—that's what they call me. The euphemism may comfort its inventor, but what woman likes the implication that she is too much? No matter how you say it, though, there aren't enough jobs. Four days before the school year starts, I still don't know if I'll be teaching.

Just when I've resigned myself to looking for another kind of work, I get the call. "You've been placed," my principal trumpets. Staffing is a complicated chess game. Unlike his other duties, such as meeting with parents or maintaining morale, it is one he excels at. "You're with us again."

I meet him in his spacious office. Tall, white-bearded, imposing, he dominates an enormous oak desk. The vice-principal, leaner and athletic, stands. They offer me coffee. As usual, it is cold and stale.

"Now that we've got you a job, what extracurricular activities are you planning to get involved in?"

"I'll run the Writers' Club."

"Good." They nod.

"And I'm going to help with the debating team."

"Excellent." They pause. The principal tugs his beard. "What else?"

What else? My assignment will be difficult. New teachers

typically get the classes no one else wants—kids who will never go on to college or university, kids who will be lucky to graduate or to qualify for any job in today's economy, kids who struggle to read. Kids who are, in another of those eloquent euphemisms, "seriously at risk." However good my intentions, however noble my aims, for most of our hours together I will be shouting myself hoarse and confiscating water pistols—and worse. Evenings, I'll grade papers, phone parents to track down truants and scramble through files searching for activities to satisfy short attention spans. What does he mean, what else? Aren't two extracurriculars on top of all that enough?

Evidently not.

"What about cheerleading?" he says.

"Cheerleading? No."

They stare. A grim-faced Santa and his unlikely elf. How can I refuse this gift they are delivering?

"I don't know anything about it."

The VP smiles. "You'll learn."

"I haven't done the First Aid course."

"Not a problem."

"But I'm opposed to cheerleading. I don't even like football!" I back up, stumble on the carpet's seam. Coffee sloshes against the side of my cracked mug. "I'm not the right person for this."

The principal frowns. "We just need someone to go to the games. You won't have to go to all the practices."

The scale feels like ice against her feet. Watching the needle balance itself, she smiles. One pound less than yesterday. Five pounds less than last week. At lunch she buys no-fat yogurt and swallows it slowly, slowly, her spine pulled straight and her stomach sucked in tight as she watches the other girls, the weak ones, scarfing down chips and chocolate. At night, she bakes. Trays of muffins, jarfuls of cookies, rich, dense cakes that she herself never touches. On her skin, the shimmer of fur, like the down on

a newborn bird. Size six, size four—all her clothes are loose on
her. She bundles them on, in layers. To keep out the terrible cold.

Tryouts take place in the playground of the neighboring elementary school. Over a hundred girls show up, all shapes, sizes and degrees of prettiness. Donna Wall, guidance secretary, golf fanatic and mother to two girls on the team, plants herself midfield and bellows names, checking them off on her clipboard. Our first job is to sort them—junior or senior, novice or expert, big enough for the base of the pyramid or small enough for its top. A few girls hang back on the edges of the crowd, taking stock of the competition, and then slink away before warm-ups begin. But more stay to perform the absurd set of kicks, jumps and acrobatics we demand of them. Donna and I look on, shading our eyes with tanned hands. I'm surprised at how often and how easily we agree. After all, what do I know about this? I've always hated cheerleaders. Yet here I am, colluding in this strange selection process: That one has energy, this one doesn't smile enough, that one might develop if we gave her a chance, this one was captain of last year's team. And she looks like trouble. Yes. No. Maybe. Yes. No.

Meanwhile, the experienced show off. Small, incredibly slender girls perch on the shoulders or the stiffly outstretched fists of slightly bigger girls. They smile; they unclip and re-clip their ponytails. The scent of their fruit shampoo and the sounds of their nervous laughter float on the late summer breeze.

Asked why they want to join the team, some girls sound vague. "I don't know. I heard the announcement." Others bridle defensively: "It's hard work, you know! You have to be really athletic!" An honest and unguarded few simply shrug and admit that their friends persuaded them to come along.

Just by attending a tryout, a girl signals her desire to belong, to fit, to be approved of by grownups and peers. Cheerleaders are so pretty in their socks and abbreviated skirts. Cheerleaders are so earnest, are such strangers to contemporary irony. Not for them the piercings, the tattoos, the black lipstick or the disaffected sneer. Cheerleaders are good girls. Such good girls.

Someone else has left her tracks. Footprints checker the toilet seat. Standing on it, you get a view of your thighs, your ass, otherwise impossible to see in the half-height mirror of this narrow bathroom. She does not bother to wipe the dust away. Instead, she bends, scanning the other stalls to see if anyone is there. No time to waste. Someone could come in at any minute.

Kneeling, she spends so much time kneeling it's a wonder she hasn't formed calluses there, or scars, like the ones that speckle the knuckles of her right hand. The concrete wall feels cool to her forehead, cool and damp. She steadies herself, then plunges her fingers down her throat. Everything comes up, everything—each greasy wheel of pepperoni, each prickly gulp of Diet Coke. She waits until she sees green—the lime green of new leaves. It is the peel of the Granny Smith she ate first, just for this purpose. So she'd know when there was nothing left inside her. So she'd know she was empty. Empty.

We're the girls from Country High
Our mothers still bake apple pie!
You think it's easy to milk a cow?
Well, listen up! We'll show you how.

Kelsey-Ann, who leads this chant, also wrote it and choreographed its accompanying moves. She captains the senior team and counsels and advises the juniors. Cheerleading is her life. But the hint of self-parody in her rhyme is intentional.

Kelsey-Ann is bright, destined for a first-class university. Small, skinny, with a squirrel-like, piquant face, bad skin and a good brain—if it weren't for cheerleading, nobody would notice her. Instead, she is one of the school's most popular girls.

No one can say she doesn't work for it. At our school, teams meet every day of the week except Friday, when games are held, and twice on Wednesday. Often on weekends, too. Football and other competitive sports get precedence, so the girls practice on the nearby elementary school playground instead of the high school playing field; on rainy days they are forced to use the cafeteria, with its dangerously low ceilings and adamantine floors, rather than the much safer gym, where the boys' teams all work out.

Cheerleading does not do wonders for the average adolescent's character. The year I coach, our team requires new uniforms. Together, we pore over catalogs. The girls sigh over the pom-poms, batons, spangles, sequins, megaphones and other accoutrements deemed unnecessary—and far too expensive.

"Short skirts," they insist. "Tight tops!"

Donna and I roll our eyes. We're thinking of more practical alternatives—elastic waists, baggy shorts, sweats—forgiving clothes that will flatter different body types. The girls will have none of it. Though they cluck their tongues in dismay at those other girls, the ones who starve themselves to stay thin, they nevertheless skip breakfast, religiously refuse that second portion. And if Jane and Shawna will look silly in skimpy skirts—well, that's just too bad. Serves them right for making such pigs of themselves. They give the team a bad image.

Nor do they want to pay for the uniforms we order. Walking around practice with a slip of paper and a moneybox, I gain new sympathy for Fuller Brush men. The look of boredom and disgust that falls across the faces of these girls is a slammed door. Their veneer of respect for me cracks and chips away—in their hearts they know I was never one of them. Their excuses aren't even creative. "My mom forgot." "I didn't get paid." "I'll have it next week." "Why do we have to pay, anyway? It's not fair!"

Whining is their characteristic pitch. To the rest of the school they look like a whirling red and gold spun-sugar fantasy, but Donna and I see them differently. Not a practice goes by without one clutch of girls refusing to participate, another group pointing fingers and telling tales, and still another group huddling in a corner, claiming illness or emotional trauma.

The seniors are the worst. "Come on!" Kelsey-Ann hollers at them. Later, she pleads, "You guys!" The whispers go on, unabated, until she slumps in a corner, admitting defeat. On the advice of a rival coach, Donna buys a large whistle, but even its shriek fails to hold the girls' attention. The only thing uniting them is their hatred of the other schools' teams. "Those hos," they sneer. "Stupid sluts."

People are astonished to hear that I'm supervising the team. "You hate that stuff!" But one friend, a poet, is more accepting and philosophical. I visit her in the city. Over wine and pasta and coffee, she listens to my complaints, extemporizing:

We're the girls from Country High.
Our mothers still bake apple pie.
Our fathers still fuck baby sheep.
At least our mothers get some sleep!

She chooses a serrated knife. Its blade feels cool against her finger, hot and cool against her arm. Her arm—apple-blossom white, rivered with blue veins and etched with the scratches and scabs from the other times, the scars she hides with long sleeves, even in the summer. One cut is not enough. The pain not sharp enough, not deep enough to shock her awake. So she cuts again, and again, pulling the blade like a saw, deeper each time, until a jagged tide of blood spills onto the kitchen countertop. She watches, pupils expanding, as the blood pools, darker, darker. Then she shakes herself and reaches for a dishcloth. To wipe away the mess.

Not everyone can make the cheerleading team. The girls I teach don't even try. Sabrina, for instance. Day after day she shuffles into class just before the bell, eyes downcast, shoulders hunched, chin angled toward her chest. Every time I speak to her, she tilts her head away and stares at the floor. I ask the other teachers about her. "What do you know about her family life? Who are her friends? Is she okay?" They shrug. She's passing her courses, barely—"at the borderline," we like to say—and she is never, never disruptive. A good girl, as bad girls go. No one considers her a problem.

Most bad girls aren't as quiet as Sabrina. Some are boisterous, bawdy, wild. But even as they thumb their noses at authority, they covertly glance at their nails to make sure their manicures are intact.

IN A SPECIAL writing class for failing students, I work with Candy. Her regular teacher tells me she is vulnerable, "running with a bad crowd," "making poor choices." When I ask Candy to write about Fridays, she considers me from beneath thick-penciled lids.

"Really?"

What Candy likes about Fridays, I discover, is being with her friends and doing all the "bad" things teenagers typically do—smoking cigarettes, drinking, taking drugs and "doing blackouts."

I think I know what a blackout is. You breathe fast, hyper-ventilate, hold your breath. Pass out.

"That's right." She grins. "Just for a minute or two."

"Does it hurt? Is it dangerous?"

"Nah," she scoffs. Later, though, she tells me that she's heard it kills brain cells.

I've always thought that blackouts were a prepubescent thrill. I'm surprised that somebody Candy's age—fourteen—would still admit to enjoying them. I ask her if everybody does.

"No. Not everybody. Just some people. My friends."

"Boys, too?"

"Oh no!" She laughs. How could I be so out of it? "Boys never do blackouts."

At this school, at least, blackouts are practiced exclusively by girls. Few methods of silencing the self could be more eloquent.

NINTH GRADE. AN unfamiliar walk through an unfamiliar part of town. Unfamiliar halls, lockers, stairwells, bodies, boys. They are bigger than my father. The school is two stories tall, and around the central foyer is a balcony where the senior boys hang out. From there they get a good view down the gaping blouses of the girls below.

Eighth grade had been a bad year. I got no invitations to par-ties, no phone calls in the evenings or on the weekends. At the graduation party, I hid in the kitchenette with the parent chaper-ones. "Such a nice girl. Such a good girl," they later told my mother.

I may be nice. I may be good. But I'm not stupid. This new year in a new school offers me my best opportunity to become somebody else, and I need to do it now, before my old repu-tation spreads. My mission is not for the faint-hearted. I wear dark, hexagonal glasses that disguise my single decent feature and dominate my pale face. I keep my bangs long to hide the pimples on my forehead. But I do know how to turn a cartwheel. I decide to try out for cheerleading.

The new gym is rank with the smell of old sweat. Running shoes squeak across the vinyl floor. The teacher, with her marbled thighs and square jaw, orders us into formation, commands us to shout our names and birthdates. "Why are gym teachers always fat and ugly," Shannon asks. She has agreed to come along for this, but when we get there, she chickens out. "Sue. You're embarrassing me," she says, as I belt out the school cheer.

For years, my mother has been telling me to keep my voice down. This is my chance to yell. But I don't yell loud enough. Or my cartwheel isn't as good as I imagine. Or something. I don't even make the first cut.

ON THE RADIO, I once heard some prominent women interviewed about their history as cheerleaders. Some said they had joined the team for fun, for excitement. Some said they wanted power. And cheerleaders do have power. Despite their low priority in the allocation of practice space, they remain the queens of the school, included on everybody's invitation list, indulged by their teachers and their classmates.

Yet this power does not come without a price. Cheerleading can be understood as a metaphor for the roles that patriarchy assigns to women. Within a patriarchal culture, all women are supposed to stand on the sidelines, support men and "build up" their accomplishments, while our own skills go uncelebrated. Within a patriarchal culture, all women, like cheerleaders, are expected to accept our subordinate position both explicitly, through our words and gestures, and implicitly, through our bodies, which are diminished and trivialized.

A strange power, that makes us small and relegates us to the margins.

SEVENTEEN STORIES IN the sky, I look out my window at blinking city lights, blurry now through the tears I cannot stop. I am twenty going on thirty-five, as my mother likes to say, but inside I am twelve—a young twelve—and tonight I might as well be two. There is no one in the world I trust.

I've been fighting with my boyfriend. In this room, in my presence, he flirted with another girl, a friend of my best friend. Angie is tall, slender, dressed in a snake-green, skin-tight dress, her long blond hair angled over an elegant eyebrow. She used to be a cheerleader, my friend says—and it shows. When Angie speaks, she sucks up all the attention in the room. When Angie moves, she sucks up all the air.

She is gone now. My boyfriend is gone, too, but he left with my insults in his ear. I said cruel things, and meant them, then, but now I am alone. Sitting on my bed, I rock, seeking refuge in the motion. Sobs rattle my frame. Tomorrow I'll find a speckled rash on my puffy face where the salt of my tears has burnt it. As if I were allergic to my own tears; as if I were allergic to myself.

I pick up my left arm, an arm I scarcely recognize. It is winter, and my wrist is pale. I twist it and stare at its underside. Hoping to stifle my sobs, I stuff it in my mouth. But the sobs go on, my frustration peaks, and watching myself, as if from afar, I bite. My teeth are strong and sharp, and the skin on my wrist is fragile. It does not hurt. I do not feel. I bite down, harder and harder. I will bring myself down to size.

What stops me, at last? I don't know. My apartment is one room. I could walk three paces for a knife, a pair of scissors. Instead, I pull back. The skin is torn in two or three spots. The air feels cool on the welts. For a week I will tug at my sleeves to disguise the raw ellipse.

"Borderline" is the name that psychiatrists give to this behavior. Borderline patients are not popular. Their problems resist treatment. Their problems seem so much their fault. They are so empty and so absent from themselves. So contrary, so confusing, so insecure, so manipulative. Like everyone's worst stereotype of "woman." No wonder, then, that the label is so rarely applied to men. Borderline, sideline, neither here nor there. Borderline, where even the cheerleaders stand.

NOVEMBER. TIME FOR my performance evaluation. The principal comes to my classes. He doesn't bother to say hello or goodbye. He sits at the back of the room in jacket and tie, his big bulk wedged into the small desk. Expressionless, he types on his laptop throughout the lessons. I'm nervous and the students are nervous; no matter how many times I've told them he'll be watching me, still they worry that he's come to judge them. Each class he attends is marked by strange mistakes on their part and on mine. I'm certain I'll get a bad report.

Instead, he gives a glowing commendation, describing me as an agreeable colleague, a co-operative junior, a "good sport," a "team player." Having taken on the cheerleaders, he means.

> Shhh. Not so loud! Hold your stomach in. Don't touch. Keep your hands to yourself. Look at the mess you've made! Don't talk with your mouth full. Don't talk back. Are you sure you want those seconds? Do as you're told. Why? Because I said so. I've had just about enough of you. I've had it, up to here.

We are such good girls. We are all of us such good girls.

SETTLING DOWN

Scott Russell Sanders

TWO FRIENDS ARRIVED at our house for supper one May evening along with the first rumblings of thunder. As Ruth and I sat talking with them on our front porch, we had to keep raising our voices a notch to make ourselves heard above the gathering storm. The birds, more discreet, had already hushed. The huge elm beside our door began to sway, limbs creaking, leaves hissing. Black sponges of clouds blotted up the light, fooling the street lamps into coming on early. Above the trees and rooftops, the murky southern sky crackled with lightning. Now and again we heard the pop of a transformer as a bolt struck the power lines in our neighborhood. The pulses of thunder came faster and faster, until they merged into a continuous roar.

We gave up on talking. The four of us, all Midwesterners teethed on thunderstorms, sat down there on the porch to our meal of lentil soup, cheddar cheese, bread warm from the oven, sliced apples and strawberries. We were lifting the first spoonfuls to our mouths when a stroke of lightning burst so nearby that it seemed to suck away the air, and the lights flickered out, plunging the whole street into darkness.

After we had caught our breath, we laughed—respectfully, as one might laugh at the joke of a giant. The sharp smell of ozone and the musty smell of damp earth mingled with the aroma of bread. A chill of pleasure ran up my spine. I lit a pair of candles on the table, and the flames rocked in the gusts of wind.

In the time it took for butter to melt on a slice of bread, the wind fell away, the elm stopped thrashing, the lightning let up, and the thunder ceased. The sudden stillness was more exciting than the earlier racket. A smoldering yellow light came into the sky, as though the humid air had caught fire. We gazed at one another over the steady candle flames and knew without exchanging a word what this eerie lull could mean.

"Maybe we should go into the basement," Ruth suggested.

"And leave this good meal?" one of our friends replied.

The wail of a siren broke the stillness—not the lesser cry of ambulance or fire engine or squad car, but the banshee howl of the civil defense siren at the park a few blocks away.

"They must have sighted one," I said.

"We could take the food down with us on a tray," Ruth told our guests.

"It's up to you," I told them. "We can go to the basement like sensible people, or we can sit here like fools and risk our necks."

"What do you want to do?" one of them asked me.

"You're the guests."

"You're the hosts."

"I'd like to stay here and see what comes," I told them.

Ruth frowned at me, but there we stayed, savoring our food and the sulphurous light. Eventually the siren quit. When my ears stopped ringing, I could hear the rushing of a great wind, like the whoosh of a waterfall. An utter calm stole over me. The hair on my neck bristled. My nostrils flared. Heat rose in my face as though the tip of a wing had raked over it.

Although I found myself, minutes later, still in the chair, the faces of my wife and friends gleaming in the candlelight, for a spell I rode the wind, dissolved into it, and there was only the great wind, rushing.

The tornado missed us by half a mile. It did not kill anyone in our vicinity, but it ripped off chimneys, toyed with cars, and plucked up a fat old maple by the roots.

Prudent folks would have gone to the basement. I do not recommend our decision; I merely report it. Why the others tarried on the porch I cannot say, but what kept me there was a mixture of curiosity and awe. I had never seen the whirling black funnel except in cautionary films, where it left a wake of havoc and tears. And now here was that tremendous power, paying us a visit. When a god comes calling, no matter how bad its reputation, would you go hide? If the siren had announced the sighting of a dragon, I would have sat there just the same, hoping to catch a glimpse of the spiked tail or fiery breath.

AS A BOY in Ohio I knew a farm family, the Millers, who not only saw but suffered from three tornadoes. The father, mother, and two sons were pulling into their driveway after church when the first tornado hoisted up their mobile home, spun it around, and carried it off. With the insurance money, they built a small frame house on the same spot. Several years later, a second tornado peeled off the roof, splintered the garage, and rustled two cows. The younger of the sons, who was in my class at school, told me that he had watched from the barn as the twister passed through, "And it never even mussed up my hair." The Millers rebuilt again, raising a new garage on the old foundation and adding another story to the house. That upper floor was reduced to kindling by a third tornado, which also pulled out half the apple trees and slurped water from the stock pond. Soon after that I left Ohio, snatched away by college as forcefully as by any cyclone. Last thing I heard, the family was preparing to rebuild yet again.

Why did the Millers refuse to budge? I knew them well enough to say they were neither stupid nor crazy. After the garage disappeared, the father hung a sign from the mailbox that read: TORNADO ALLEY. He figured the local terrain would coax future whirlwinds in their direction. Then why not move? Plain stubbornness was a factor. These were people who, once settled, might have remained at the foot of a volcano or on the bank of a flood-prone river or beside an earthquake fault. They had relatives nearby, helpful neighbors, jobs and stores and school within a short drive, and those were all good reasons to stay. But the main reason, I believe, was because the Millers had invested so much of their lives in the land, planting orchards and gardens, spreading manure on the fields, digging ponds, building sheds, seeding pastures. Out back of the house were groves of walnuts, hickories, and oaks, all started by hand from acorns and nuts. Honeybees zipped out from a row of white hives to nuzzle clover in the pasture. April through October, perennial flowers in the yard pumped out a fountain of blossoms. This farm was not just so many acres of dirt, easily exchanged for an equal amount elsewhere; it was a particular place, intimately known, worked on, dreamed over, cherished.

Psychologists tell us that we answer trouble with one of two impulses, either fight or flight. I believe that the Millers' response to tornadoes and my own keen expectancy on the porch arose from a third instinct, that of staying put. When the pain of leaving behind what we know outweighs the pain of embracing it, or when the power we face is overwhelming and neither fight nor flight will save us, there may be salvation in sitting still. And if salvation is impossible, then at least before perishing we may gain a clearer vision of where we are. By sitting still I do not mean the paralysis of dread, like that of a rabbit frozen beneath the dive of a hawk. I mean something like reverence, a respectful waiting, a deep attentiveness to forces much greater than our own. If indulged only for a moment, as in my case on the porch, this reverent impulse may amount to little; but if sustained for months and years, as by the Millers on their farm, it may yield marvels. The Millers knew better than to fight a tornado, and they chose not to flee. Instead they devoted themselves, season after season, to patient labor. Instead of withdrawing, they gave themselves more fully. Their commitment to the place may have been foolhardy, but it was also grand. I suspect that most human achievements worth admiring are the result of such devotion.

These tornado memories dramatize a choice we are faced with constantly: whether to go or stay, whether to move to a situation that is safer, richer, easier, more attractive, or to stick where we are and make what we can of it. If the shine goes off our marriage, our house, our car, do we trade it for a new one? If the fertility leaches out of our soil, the creativity out of our job, the money out of our pocket, do we start over somewhere else? There are voices enough, both inner and outer, urging us to deal with difficulties by pulling up stakes and heading for new territory. I know them well, for they have been calling to me all my days. I wish to raise here a contrary voice, to say a few words on behalf of standing your ground, confronting the powers, going deeper.

IN A POEM written not long before he leapt from a bridge over the Mississippi River, John Berryman ridiculed those who asked about his "roots" ("as if I were a *plant*"), and he articulated something like a credo for the dogma of rootlessness:

> *Exile is in our time like blood. Depend on*
> *interior journeys taken anywhere.*

I'd rather live in Venice or Kyoto,
except for the languages, but
O really I don't care where I live or have lived.
Wherever I am, young Sir, my wits about me,

memory blazing, I'll cope & make do.

It is a bold claim, but also a hazardous one. For all his wits, Berryman in the end failed to cope well enough to stave off suicide. The truth is, none of us can live by wits alone. For even the barest existence, we depend on the labors of other people, the fruits of the earth, the inherited goods of our given place. If our interior journeys are cut loose entirely from that place, then both we and the neighborhood will suffer.

Exile usually suggests banishment, a forced departure from one's homeland. Famines and tyrants and wars do indeed force entire populations to flee; but most people who move, especially within the industrialized world, do so by choice. Salman Rushdie chose to leave his native India for England, where he has written a series of brilliant books from the perspective of a cultural immigrant. Like many writers, he has taken his own condition to represent not merely a possibility but a norm. In the essays of *Imaginary Homelands* he celebrates "the migrant sensibility," whose development he regards as "one of the central themes of this century of displaced persons." Rushdie has also taken this condition to represent something novel in history:

The effect of mass migrations has been the creation of radically new types of human being: people who root themselves in ideas rather than places, in memories as much as in material things;

*people who have been obliged to define themselves—because
they are so defined by others—by their otherness; people in
whose deepest selves strange fusions occur, unprecedented unions
between what they were and where they find themselves.*

In the history of America, that description applies just as
well to the Pilgrims in Plymouth, say, or to Swiss homesteading
in Indiana, to Chinese trading in California, to former slaves
crowding into cities on the Great Lakes, or to Seminoles driven
onto reservations a thousand miles from their traditional land.
Displaced persons are abundant in our century, but hardly a
novelty.

Claims for the virtues of shifting ground are familiar and
seductive to Americans, this nation of restless movers. From
the beginning, our heroes have been sailors, explorers, cowboys,
prospectors, speculators, backwoods ramblers, rainbowchasers,
vagabonds of every stripe. Our Promised Land has always been
over the next ridge or at the end of the trail, never under our
feet. One hundred years after the official closing of the frontier,
we have still not shaken off the romance of unlimited space. If
we fish out a stream or wear out a field, or if the smoke from a
neighbor's chimney begins to crowd the sky, why, off we go to
a new stream, a fresh field, a clean sky. In our national mythology, the worst fate is to be trapped on a farm, in a village, in
the sticks, in some dead-end job or unglamorous marriage or
played-out game. Stand still, we are warned, and you die. Americans have dug the most canals, laid the most rails, built the most
roads and airports of any nation. In the newspaper I read that,
even though our sprawling system of interstate highways is
crumbling, the president has decided that we should triple it in
size, and all without raising our taxes a nickel. Only a populace
drunk on driving, a populace infatuated with the myth of the

open road, could hear such a proposal without hooting.

So Americans are likely to share Rushdie's enthusiasm for migration, for the "hybridity, impurity, intermingling, the transformation that comes of new and unexpected combinations of human beings, cultures, ideas, politics, movies, songs." Everything about us is mongrel, from race to language, and we are stronger for it. Yet we might respond more skeptically when Rushdie says that "to be a migrant is, perhaps, to be the only species of human being free of the shackles of nationalism (to say nothing of its ugly sister, patriotism)." Lord knows we could do with less nationalism (to say nothing of its ugly siblings, racism, religious sectarianism, or class snobbery). But who would pretend that a history of migration has immunized the United States against bigotry? And even if, by uprooting ourselves, we shed our chauvinism, is that all we lose?

In this hemisphere, many of the worst abuses—of land, forests, animals, and communities—have been carried out by "people who root themselves in ideas rather than places." Rushdie claims that "migrants must, of necessity, make a new imaginative relationship with the world, because of the loss of familiar habitats." But migrants often pack up their visions and values with the rest of their baggage and carry them along. The Spaniards devastated Central and South America by imposing on this New World the religion, economics, and politics of the Old. Colonists brought slavery with them to North America, along with smallpox and Norway rats. The Dust Bowl of the 1930s was caused not by drought but by the transfer onto the Great Plains of farming methods that were suitable to wetter regions. The habit of our industry and commerce has been to force identical schemes onto differing locales, as though the mind were a cookie-cutter and the land were dough.

I quarrel with Rushdie because he articulates as eloquently

as anyone the orthodoxy that I wish to counter: the belief that movement is inherently good, staying put is bad; that uprooting brings tolerance, while rootedness breeds intolerance; that imaginary homelands are preferable to geographical ones; that to be modern, enlightened, fully of our time is to be displaced. Wholesale displacement may be inevitable; but we should not suppose that it occurs without disastrous consequences for the earth and for ourselves. People who root themselves in places are likelier to know and care for those places than are people who root themselves in ideas. When we cease to be migrants and become inhabitants, we might begin to pay enough heed and respect to where we are. By settling in, we have a chance of making a durable home for ourselves, our fellow creatures and our descendants.

WHAT ARE WE up against, those of us who aspire to become inhabitants, who wish to commit ourselves to a place? How strong, how old, is the impulse we are resisting?

Although our machines enable us to move faster and farther, humans have been on the move for a long time. Within a few clicks on the evolutionary clock, our ancestors roamed out of their native valleys in Africa and spread over the Eurasian continent. They invaded the deserts, the swamps, the mountains and valleys, the jungle and tundra. Drifting on boats and rafts, they pushed on to island after island around the globe. When glaciers locked up enough sea water to expose a land bridge from Asia to North America, migrants crossed into this unknown region, and within a few thousand years their descendants had scattered from the Bering Straits to Tierra del Fuego.

The mythology of those first Americans often claimed that a tribe had been attached to a given spot since the beginning of time, and we in our craving for rootedness may be inclined to believe in this eternal bond between people and place; but archaeology suggests that ideas, goods, and populations were in motion for millennia before the first Europeans reached these shores, hunters and traders and whole tribes roving about, boundaries shifting, homelands changing hands. Even agricultural settlements, such as those associated with the mound-building cultures in the Mississippi and Ohio Valleys, reveal a history of arrivals and departures, sites used for decades or centuries and then abandoned. By comparison to our own hectic movements, an association between people and place lasting decades or centuries may seem durable and enviable; but it is not eternal.

What I am saying is that we are a wandering species, and have been since we reared up on our hind legs and stared at the horizon. Our impulse to wander, to pick up and move when things no longer suit us in our present place, is not an ailment brought on suddenly by industrialization, by science, or by the European hegemony over dark-skinned peoples. It would be naive to think that Spanish horses corrupted the Plains Indians, tempting a sedentary people to rush about, or that snowmobiles corrupted the Inuit, or that Jeeps corrupted the Aborigines. It would be just as naive to say that the automobile gave rise to our own restlessness; on the contrary, our restlessness gave rise to the automobile, as it led to the bicycle, steamboat, and clipper ship, as it led to the taming of horses, lacing of snowshoes, and carving of dugout canoes.

Our itch to wander was the great theme of the English writer Bruce Chatwin, who died in 1989 from a rare disease contracted in the course of his own incessant travels. For Chatwin, "the nature of human restlessness" was "the question of questions." One hundred pages of The Songlines, his best-known work, are filled with notebook entries supporting the view that "man is a migratory species." In a posthumous collection of essays entitled *What Am I Doing Here*, he summed up his observations:

> [W]e should perhaps allow human nature an appetitive drive for movement in the widest sense. The act of journeying contributes towards a sense of physical and mental well-being, while the monotony of prolonged settlement or regular work weaves patterns in the brain that engender fatigue and a sense of personal inadequacy. Much of what the ethologists have designated "aggression" is simply an angered response to the frustrations of confinement.

I am dubious about the psychology here, for I notice Chatwin's own frustrations in the passage, especially in that irritable phrase about "the monotony of prolonged settlement or regular work;" but I agree with his speculation that deep in us there is "an appetitive drive for movement."

The movement chronicled in *The Songlines*—the purposeful wandering of the Australian Aborigines—may suggest a way for us to harness our restlessness, a way to reconcile our need to rove with our need to settle down. As hunter-gatherers in a harsh continent, the Aborigines must know their land thoroughly and travel it widely in order to survive. According to their belief, the land and all living things were created in a mythic time called the Dreaming, and the creative spirits are still at work, sustaining the world. Humans keep the world in touch with the power of the Dreaming by telling stories and singing songs. The whole of Australia is crisscrossed by pathways known to the Aborigines, who must walk them at intervals, performing the songs that belong to each path. Every tribe is responsible for the tracks within its own territory, and for passing down the appropriate songs from generation to generation. "There was hardly a rock or creek in the country," Chatwin remarks, "that could not or had not been sung." The movement of the Aborigines is not random, therefore, but deliberate, guided by hunger and thirst, but also by the need to participate in the renewal of the world. The land supplies the necessities of life, and in return humans offer knowledge, memory, and voice.

The Aboriginal walkabout illustrates "the once universal concept," in Chatwin's words, "that wandering re-establishes the original harmony…between man and the universe." Unlike vagabonds, who use up place after place without returning on their tracks, the Aborigines wed themselves to one place, and range over it with gratitude and care. So that they might continue as residents, they become stewards. Like the rest of nature, they move in circles, walking again and again over sacred ground.

THE AUSTRALIAN ABORIGINES are among the "inhabitory peoples" whom Gary Snyder has studied in his search for wisdom about living in place, a wisdom he described in The Old Ways:

> People developed specific ways to be in each of those niches: plant knowledge, boats, dogs, traps, nets, fishing—the smaller animals, and smaller tools. From steep jungle slopes of Southwest China to coral atolls to barren arctic deserts—a spirit of what it was to be there evolved, that spoke of a direct sense of relation to the "land"—which really means, the totality of the local bio-region system, from cirrus clouds to leaf-mold.

Such knowledge does not come all at once; it accumulates bit by bit over generations, each person adding to the common lore.

Even nomads, whose name implies motion, must be scholars

of their bioregion. As they follow herds from pasture to pasture through the cycle of the year, they trace a loop that is dictated by what the land provides. For inhibitory peoples, listening to the land is a spiritual discipline as well as a practical one. The alertness that feeds the body also feeds the soul. In Native American culture, "medicine" is understood not as a human invention, but as a channeling of the power by which all things live. Whether you are a hunter-gatherer, a nomad, a farmer, or a suburbanite, to be at home in the land is to be sane and whole.

The Aborigines worked out an accommodation with their land over 40,000 years, no doubt through trial and error. They would not have survived if their mythology had not soon come to terms with their ecology. Even so, their population was never more than about one hundredth as large as that of modern Australia. We who live in North America are engaged in our own trials and errors, which are greatly magnified by the size of our population and the power of our technology. A man with a bulldozer can make a graver mistake in one day than a whole tribe with digging sticks can make in a year. In my home region, mistakes are being made seven days a week—with machinery, chemicals, guns, plows, fountain pens, bare hands. I suspect the same is true in every region. But who is keeping track? Who speaks for the wordless creatures? Who supplies memory and conscience for the land?

Half a century ago, in A Sand County Almanac, Aldo Leopold gave us an ecological standard for judging our actions: "A thing is right when it tends to preserve the integrity, stability, and beauty of the biotic community. It is wrong when it tends otherwise." We can only apply that standard if, in every biotic community, there are residents who keep watch over what is preserved and what is lost, who see the beauty that escapes the frame of the tourist's windshield or the investor's spreadsheet. "The problem,"

Leopold observed, "is how to bring about a striving for harmony with land among a people many of whom have forgotten there is any such thing as land, among whom education and culture have become almost synonymous with landlessness."

The question is not whether land belongs to us, through titles registered in a courthouse, but whether we belong to the land, through our loyalty and awareness. In the preface to his *The Natural History and Antiquities of Selborne*, the eighteenth-century English vicar, Gilbert White, notes that a comprehensive survey of England might be compiled if only "stationary men would pay some attention to the districts on which they reside." Every township, every field and creek, every mountain and forest on Earth would benefit from the attention of stationary men and women. No one has understood this need better than Gary Snyder:

> One of the key problems in American society now, it seems to me, is people's lack of commitment to any given place—which, again, is totally unnatural and outside of history. Neighborhoods are allowed to deteriorate, landscapes are allowed to be strip-mined, because there is nobody who will live there and take responsibility; they'll just move on. The reconstruction of a people and of a life in the United States depends in part on people, neighborhood by neighborhood, county by county, deciding to stick it out and make it work where they are, rather than flee.

We may not have forty years, let alone 40,000, to reconcile our mythology with our ecology. If we are to reshape our way of thinking to fit the way of things, as the songs of the Aborigines follow their terrain, many more of us need to know our local ground, walk over it, care for it, fight for it, bear it steadily in mind.

BUT IF YOU stick in one place, won't you become a stick-in-the-mud? If you stay put, won't you be narrow, backward, dull? You might. I have met ignorant people who never moved; and I have also met ignorant people who never stood still. Committing yourself to a place does not guarantee that you will become wise, but neither does it guarantee that you will become parochial. Who knows better the limitations of a province or a culture than the person who has bumped into them time and again? The history of settlement in my own district and the continuing abuse of land hereabouts provoke me to rage and grief. I know the human legacy here too well to glamorize it.

To become intimate with your home region, to know the territory as well as you can, to understand your life as woven into the local life does not prevent you from recognizing and honoring the diversity of other places, cultures, ways. On the contrary, how can you value other places if you do not have one of your own? If you are not yourself *placed*, then you wander the world like a sightseer, a collector of sensations, with no gauge for measuring what you see. Local knowledge is the grounding for global knowledge. Those who care about nothing beyond the confines of their parish are in truth parochial, and are at least mildly dangerous to their *parish*; on the other hand, those who have no parish, those who navigate ceaselessly among postal zones and area codes, those for whom the world is only a smear of highways and bank accounts and stores, are a danger not just to their parish but to the planet.

Since birth, my children have been surrounded by images of the earth as viewed from space, images that I first encountered when I was in my twenties. Those photographs show vividly what in our sanest moments we have always known—that the earth is a closed circle, lovely and rare. On the wall beside me as I write there is a poster of the big blue marble encased in its white swirl of clouds. That is one pole of my awareness; but the other pole is what I see through my window. I try to keep both in sight at once.

For all my convictions, I still have to wrestle with the fear—in myself, in my children, and in some of my neighbors—that our place is too remote from the action. This fear drives many people to pack their bags and move to some resort or burg they have seen on television, leaving behind what they learn to think of as the boondocks. I deal with my own unease by asking just what action I am remote from—a stock market? a debating chamber? a drive-in mortuary? The action that matters, the work of nature and community, goes on everywhere.

Since Copernicus we have known better than to see the earth as the center of the universe. Since Einstein, we have learned that there is no center; or alternatively, that any point is as good as any other for observing the world. I take this to be roughly what medieval theologians meant when they defined God as a circle whose circumference is nowhere and whose center is everywhere. I find a kindred lesson in the words of the Zen master, Thich Nhat Hanh: "This spot where you sit is your own spot. It is on this very spot and in this very moment that you can become enlightened. You don't have to sit beneath a special tree in a distant land." There are no privileged locations. If you stay put, your place may become a holy center, not because it gives you special access to the divine, but because in your stillness you hear what might be heard anywhere. All there is to see can be seen from anywhere in the universe, if you know how to look; and the influence of the entire universe converges on every spot.

EXCEPT FOR THE rare patches of wilderness, every place on earth has been transformed by human presence. "Ecology becomes a more complex but far more interesting science," René Dubos observes in *The Wooing of Earth*, "when human aspirations are regarded as an integral part of the landscape." Through "long periods of intimate association between human beings and nature," Dubos argues, landscape may take on a "quality of blessedness." The intimacy is crucial: the understanding of how to dwell in a place arises out of a sustained conversation between people and land. When there is no conversation, when we act without listening, when we impose our desires without regard for the qualities or needs of our place, then landscape may be cursed rather than blessed by our presence.

If our fidelity to place is to help renew and preserve our neighborhoods, it will have to be informed by what Wendell Berry calls "an ecological intelligence: a sense of the impossibility of acting or living alone or solely in one's own behalf, and this rests in turn upon a sense of the order upon which any life depends and of the proprieties of place within that order." Proprieties of place: actions, words, and values that are *proper* to your home ground. I think of my home ground as a series of nested rings, with house and marriage and family at the center, surrounded by the wider and wider hoops of neighborhood and community, the bioregion within walking distance of my door, the wooded hills and karst landscape of southern Indiana, the watershed of the Ohio River, and so on outward—and inward— to the ultimate source.

The longing to become an inhabitant rather than a drifter sets me against the current of my culture, which nudges everyone into motion. Newton taught us that a body at rest tends to stay at rest, unless acted on by an outside force. We are acted on ceaselessly by outside forces—advertising, movies, magazines, speeches—and also by the inner force of biology. I am not immune to their pressure. Before settling in my present home, I lived in seven states and two countries, tugged from place to place in childhood by my father's work and in early adulthood by my own. This itinerant life is so common among the people I know that I have been slow to conceive of an alternative. Only by knocking against the golden calf of mobility, which looms so large and shines so brightly, have I come to realize that it is hollow. Like all idols, it distracts us from the true divinity.

The ecological argument for staying put may be easier for us to see than the spiritual one, worried as we are about saving our skins. Few of us worry about saving our souls, and fewer still imagine that the condition of our souls has anything to do with the condition of our neighborhoods. Talk about enlightenment makes us jittery, because it implies that we pass our ordinary days in darkness. You recall the scene in *King Lear* when blind and wretched old Gloucester, wishing to commit suicide, begs a young man to lead him to the brink of a cliff. The young man is Gloucester's son, Edgar, who fools the old man into thinking they have come to a high bluff at the edge of the sea. Gloucester kneels, then tumbles forward onto the level ground; on landing, he is amazed to find himself alive. He is transformed by the fall. Blind, at last he is able to see his life clearly; despairing, he discovers hope. To be enlightened, he did not have to leap to someplace else; he only had to come hard against the ground where he already stood.

MY FRIEND RICHARD, who wears a white collar to his job, recently bought forty acres of land that had been worn out by the standard local regimen of chemicals and corn. Evenings and weekends, he has set about restoring the soil by spreading manure, planting clover and rye, and filling the eroded gullies with brush. His pond has gathered geese, his young orchard has tempted deer, and his nesting boxes have attracted swallows and bluebirds. Now he is preparing a field for the wild flowers and prairie grasses that once flourished here. Having contemplated this work since he was a boy, Richard will not be chased away by fashions or dollars or tornadoes. On a recent airplane trip he was distracted from the book he was reading by thoughts of renewing the land. So he sketched on the flyleaf a plan of labor for the next ten years. Most of us do not have forty acres to care for, but that should not keep us from sowing and tending local crops.

I think about Richard's ten year vision when I read a report chronicling the habits of computer users who, apparently, grow impatient if they have to wait more than a second for their machine to respond. I use a computer, but I am wary of the haste it encourages. Few answers that matter will come to us in a second; some of the most vital answers will not come in a decade, or a century.

When the chiefs of the Iroquois nation sit in council, they are sworn to consider how their decisions will affect their descendants seven generations into the future. Seven generations! Imagine our politicians thinking beyond the next opinion poll, beyond the next election, beyond their own lifetimes, two centuries ahead. Imagine our bankers, our corporate executives, our advertising moguls weighing their judgments on that scale. Looking seven generations into the future, could a developer pave another farm? Could a farmer spray another pound of poison? Could the captain of an oil tanker flush his tanks at sea? Could you or I write checks and throw switches without a much greater concern for what is bought and sold, what is burned?

As I write this, I hear the snarl of earthmovers and chain saws a mile away destroying a farm to make way for another shopping strip. I would rather hear a tornado, whose damage can be undone. The elderly woman who owned the farm had it listed in the National Register, then willed it to her daughters on condition they preserve it. After her death, the daughters, who live out of state, had the will broken, so the land could be turned over to the chain saws and earthmovers. The machines work around the clock. Their noise wakes me at midnight, at three in the morning, at dawn. The roaring abrades my dreams. The sound is a reminder that we are living in the midst of a holocaust. I do not use the word lightly. The earth is being pillaged, and every one of us, willingly or grudgingly, is taking part. We ask how sensible, educated, supposedly moral people could have tolerated slavery or the slaughter of Jews. Similar questions will be asked about us by our descendants, to whom we bequeath an impoverished planet. They will demand to know how we could have been party to such waste and ruin. They will have good reason to curse our memory.

What does it mean to be alive in an era when the earth is being devoured, and in a country which has set the pattern for that devouring? What are we called to do? I think we are called to the work of healing, both inner and outer: healing of the mind through a change in consciousness, healing of the earth through a change in our lives. We can begin that work by learning how to abide in a place. I am talking about an active commitment, not a passive lingering. If you stay with a husband or wife out of laziness rather than love, that is inertia, not marriage. If you stay put through cowardice rather than conviction, you will have no strength to act. Strength comes, healing comes, from aligning yourself with the grain of your place and answering to its needs.

"The man who is often thinking that it is better to be somewhere else than where he is excommunicates himself," we are cautioned by Thoreau, that notorious stay-at-home. The metaphor is religious: to withhold yourself from where you are is to be cut off from communion with the source. It has taken me half a lifetime of searching to realize that the likeliest path to the ultimate ground leads through my local ground. I mean the land itself, with its creeks and rivers, its weather, seasons, stone outcroppings, and all the plants and animals that share it. I cannot have a spiritual center without having a geographical one; I cannot live a grounded life without being grounded in a *place*.

In belonging to a landscape, one feels a rightness, at-home-ness, a knitting of self and world. This condition of clarity and focus, this being fully present, is akin to what the Buddhists call mindfulness, what Christian contemplatives refer to as recollection, what Quakers call centering down. I am suspicious of any philosophy that would separate this-worldly from other-worldly commitment. There is only one world, and we participate in it here and now, in our flesh and our place.

THANKS

I N THIS FIRST anthology we'd like to thank all the people who have helped make this book, and Nonvella itself, possible. I'll speak in the editorial "we" voice here for both Anne Cassel-man and I, but if anyone has been left off these pages, the error belongs to me alone. And I apologize profusely.

First we'd like to thank our respective spouses, Michele Bridge and Josh Dunford, for their tremendous patience and generosity as we worked, sometimes manically and often very late, to launch this project over the past two years. Thanks go to all the authors in the pages of this anthology, and in our current and forthcoming books, who have gener-ously shared their work with us. We hope to keep ourselves to the same high standards you all set in your writing. In particular we tip a glass toward the writers of our first two stand-alone nonvellas: Timothy Taylor, author of *Foodville*, and Adam Pez, author of *The Silicon Rapture*. Thanks for taking the risk with us.

Nonvella wouldn't be here without the help of many highly intelligent, well-informed and patient advisors and assistants, known to us collectively as Team Nonvella. These include but are not limited to Zoe Grams, Jesse Finkelstein, Trena White, Alison Cairns, Peter Cocking, Carra Simpson, Janet Filipenko and Nelly Bouevitch.

For early inspiration and ongoing encouragement we thank the members of our advisory board: J.B. MacKinnon, John Vaillant, Deborah Campbell, Alisa Smith, Bruce Grierson, Charles Montgomery, Brian Payton, Erin Millar, Brian Payton, Christine McLaren, Charlotte Gill and Jennica Harper. And lastly we offer a mug-hoisting, table-rousing slainte and kanpai to all of our Kickstarter backers, large and small, for giving us the financing to get Nonvella out of our heads and onto the bookstore shelves, digitally and physically.

Our thanks to everyone for your faith in us and your support of writers, great nonfiction, and the future of publishing—wherever it takes us.

T.B.

ABOUT THE AUTHORS

J.B. MACKINNON'S latest book, *The Once and Future World* (September 2013), explores the richer, more abundant natural world of the past and what it tells us about nature today. Previous works are *The 100-Mile Diet* (with Alisa Smith), a bestseller widely recognized as a catalyst of the local foods movement; *I Live Here* (with Mia Kirshner and artists Michael Simons and Paul Shoebridge), a "paper documentary" about displaced people that made the *Bloomsbury Literary Review's* top-10 list; and *Dead Man in Paradise*, the story of a priest assassinated in the Dominican Republic, which won the Charles Taylor Prize for literary nonfiction. His recent essay "False Idyll" appears in *Best American Science and Nature Writing 2013*.

    www.jbmackinnnon.com

DEBORAH CAMPBELL is the author of *This Heated Place* and the winner of several National Magazine Awards for her foreign correspondence, as well as the Dave Greber Freelance Writers Award for her *Harper's* piece on Iraqi refugees. Her writing has been been published in ten countries and five languages.

    www.deborahcampbell.org

JAKE MACDONALD has written eight books of both fiction and non-fiction and several hundred articles for many of Canada's leading publications, including the *Globe and Mail*, *Canadian Geographic*, and *Outdoor Canada*. His book *Houseboat Chronicles* won three awards, including the Writers Trust of Canada prize for non-fiction; *Grizzlyville*, a meditation on North America's largest predators and on the people who deal with them, was published in 2009.

SUSAN OLDING is the author of *Pathologies: A Life in Essays* (Freehand, 2008), winner of the Creative Nonfiction Collective's Readers' Choice Award for 2010. Her writing has appeared widely in literary journals and anthologies across Canada and the United States, and has won a National Magazine Award and two Edna awards, among others.
www.susanolding.com

SCOTT RUSSELL SANDERS is the author of twenty books of fiction and nonfiction, including *A Private History of Awe* and *A Conservationist Manifesto*. The best of his essays from the past thirty years, plus nine new essays, are collected in *Earth Works*, published in 2012 by Indiana University Press. Among his honors are the Lannan Literary Award, the John Burroughs Essay Award, the Mark Twain Award, the Cecil Woods Award for Nonfiction, the Eugene and Marilyn Glick Indiana Authors Award, and fellowships from the Guggenheim Foundation and the National Endowment for the Arts. In 2012 he was elected to the American Academy of Arts and Sciences. His latest book is *Divine Animal*, a novel, published in 2014. He is a Distinguished Professor Emeritus of English at Indiana University, where he taught from 1971 to 2009. He and his wife, Ruth, a biochemist, have reared two children in their hometown of Bloomington, in the hardwood hill country of Indiana's White River Valley.
www.scottrussellsanders.com

Thanks for reading.

Made in the USA
Charleston, SC
14 October 2014